Autumn
Rachelle
Grangruth

The Art, the Artists, and the Story
Behind the Amazing Movie

STUART LITTLE™

The Art, the Artists, and the Story Behind the Amazing Movie

Edited by Linda Sunshine • Preface by Rob Minkoff
Screenplay by M. Night Shyamalan and Greg Brooker

A NEWMARKET PICTORIAL MOVIEBOOK

NEWMARKET PRESS
NEW YORK

This book is published in the United States of America and Canada.

All rights reserved. This book may not be reproduced, in whole or in part, in any
form, without written permission. Inquiries should be addressed to Permissions
Department, Newmarket Press, 18 East 48th Street, New York, NY 10017.

First Edition

10 9 8 7 6 5 4 3 2 1 (hardcover)
10 9 8 7 6 5 4 3 2 1 (paperback)

Library of Congress Cataloging-in-Publication Data is available upon request.

ISBN 1-55704-408-2 (hardcover)
ISBN 1-55704-407-4 (paperback)

QUANTITY PURCHASES
Companies, professional groups, clubs, and other organizations may qualify for
special terms when ordering quantities of this title. For information, write Special
Sales Department, Newmarket Press, 18 East 48th Street, New York, NY 10017;
call (212) 832-3575; fax (212) 832-3629; or email newmktprs@aol.com.

www.newmarketpress.com

Designed by Timothy Shaner

Manufactured in the United States of America

Other Newmarket Pictorial Moviebooks Include:
    *Magnolia: The Shooting Script**
    *Cradle Will Rock: The Movie and The Moment**
    Saving Private Ryan: The Men, The Mission, The Movie
    Amistad: A Celebration of the Film by Steven Spielberg
    *The Seven Years in Tibet Screenplay and Story Behind the Film**
    *Men in Black: The Script and the Story Behind the Film**
    *The Age of Innocence: A Portrait of the Film Based on the Novel by Edith Wharton**
    *The Sense and Sensibility Screenplay & Diaries**
    *Mary Shelley's Frankenstein: The Classic Tale of Terror Reborn on Film**
    *Bram Stoker's Dracula: The Film and the Legend**
    *Dances with Wolves: The Illustrated Story of the Epic Film**
    Gandhi: A Pictorial Biography
    The Inner Circle: An Inside View of Soviet Life Under Stalin
    *Neil Simon's Lost in Yonkers: The Illustrated Screenplay of the Film**
    *Wild Wild West: The Illustrated Story Behind the Film**
    *Wyatt Earp: The Film and the Filmmakers**
    **Includes Screenplay*

Visit our website at www.stuartlittle.com

Contents

PREFACE
by Rob Minkoff
6

INTRODUCTION
8

THE ILLUSTRATED SCRIPT
24

CREDITS
142

The Filmmakers
144

The Cast
152

Film Credit Roll
154

Acknowledgments
160

Preface

"A talking mouse, you say? There's nothing new in that." But where Stuart Little is concerned, you'd be mistaken. Unlike his traditionally animated brethren Mickey, Mighty, and Feival, Stuart was created using the most up-to-date computer graphic imaging (CGI) technology.

Coming from animation, as I do, the notion of a talking mouse was not surprising, but creating him for a live-action film was a challenge like no other.

People naturally assume that animated characters are easier to work with than their human counterparts. Unlike a human actor, who can question, argue, and alter your vision, an animated character can be manipulated simply by grabbing the nearest eraser. This could not be further from the truth. After all, behind every great animated character is a great animator.

The fact is, both kinds of filmmaking require a very rare species of artist. Whether it's the actor using his body, the animator a pencil, or the CGI animator a computer, all must contribute their unique gifts to the ultimate goal: telling an entertaining story about a compelling character.

—ROB MINKOFF

Rob Minkoff directing Geena Davis and Hugh Laurie on the Central Park stage.

Above: Drawing of Stuart Little by Garth Williams from the 1945 book. Right: Sketch by Thor Freudenthal of Stuart as Charlie Chaplin. Many animators study the work of great silent screen stars to learn more about portraying emotion through body movement.

DOUGLAS WICK ON THE STORY

Fifty years after E. B. White dreamed up *Stuart Little*, Columbia Pictures bought the motion picture and television rights to the book, and I had the job of trying to bring him to the big screen. That was six years ago. I didn't think it would be nearly so hard.

We had an original hero and lots of great escapades, so it seemed as if the movie would just write itself. No.

Our main problem was adapting the original story to the screen. The book is very episodic, and the first few scripts we got were just a bunch of Stuart adventures glued together but without the literate voice of E. B. White holding it all in place. We had to find a way to organize those episodes into one fluid story.

By then I was working with a very gifted screenwriter named M. Night Shyamalan, who had just written and directed *The Sixth Sense*. We turned in a new script, basically a different version of the same problem, and the Columbia executives told us that they were shutting down *Stuart*. It was over. A few days later, those executives were fired. I learned a serious lesson about being partnered with Stuart Little: The little mouse never gives up and neither should I.

While we waited for the new administration, we decided to take one more try at the script. I turned to one of my film heroes, Charlie Chaplin, and looked at his transition from two-reelers to features. It was the same journey from short episodes to a longer format that we needed to re-create. We needed a simple story like *The Kid* or *City Lights* that would dramatize some basic issue of Stuart in the world. We decided to focus on his love story with the family: Mouse meets family, mouse loses family, mouse gets family. Night went off to work and came back with the rarest of all things—a genuinely good screenplay. The new executives read *Stuart Little* and set the movie into motion.

INTRODUCTION

"For me, the theme of the movie is that everyone deserves to be loved and accepted for who they are and not what they look like."

—GEENA DAVIS

The Company That Built a Better Mouse

BY DON LEVY

Sony Pictures Imageworks was founded in 1992 on the notion that imagination unbound could lead to astonishing entertainment.

In the beginning, Imageworks was a handful of pioneers, including a young computer graphics artist named Jerome Chen. Much of the work being done during those first experimental years was in the area of pre-visualization and titling. Pre-visualizations allowed filmmakers to be more precise and accurate by using computer simulations to conceive elaborate shot sequences.

Out of those pre-visualizations, Imageworks began developing ever more successful visual effects in such films as *In the Line of Fire,* where Clint Eastwood was integrated into live-action footage of the Secret Service in action, and the famous bus jump in *Speed.*

The real transition came in 1995, when Sony Pictures Entertainment realized that Imageworks needed the commitment of the studio to ramp up operations in order to be competitive on both a technical and a creative level. Kenneth Williams, now the President of Sony Pictures Digital Studios Division, was the executive responsible for the studio's wholesale overhaul support to become Hollywood's most fully integrated digital-production facility. While much of the industry just talked about retooling their operations for the digital era, Ken Williams and the executive team at Sony Pictures put the pieces in place.

On a purely business level, the top-grossing movies of all time have one component in common: visual effects. Even films like *Gone With the Wind* and *The Wizard of Oz* dazzled audiences with spectacular images. While moviegoers' tastes change from year to year, the constant is a demand for great stories, wonderfully told. The best movies have always succeeded in taking audiences to distant lands and magical places, into adventures and on elaborate odysseys.

The vision for Imageworks was to establish itself as  a different kind of visual effects company—a filmmaker's effects company. It would be the kind of company that would push technology to its limits and make new discoveries, a company that could attract some of the most gifted of individuals and provide a place where they could unleash their talent. Perhaps most important, it would be a company founded with enormous respect for movies and moviemakers.

Five-time Academy Award winner Ken Ralston joined Imageworks at the end of 1995 to realize this artistic vision. With Ralston, the company attracted some of the world's most prominent visual effects talent, including Academy Award winners Scott E. Anderson, John Dykstra, Rob Legato, nominee Pat McClung, and Motion Picture Academy scientific and technical achievement award winners Lincoln Hu and George Joblove. Also coming onboard at this time was Barry Weiss to head up a nascent digital-character group. The company embarked on a massive project to create a state-of-the-art digital infrastructure, deploying the lat-

10

est in technical innovations to advance the art form. Within six months of Ralston's arrival, Imageworks moved into its new facilities in Culver City, California, and began work on two groundbreaking projects, *Contact,* for director Robert Zemeckis, and *Starship Troopers,* with director Paul Verhoeven.

By the time Tim Sarnoff joined Imageworks in 1997 as its Executive Vice President and General Manager, the company had established a sturdy reputation for artistic excellence. Sarnoff didn't come to Imageworks to maintain the status quo. Having spent nearly a decade at Warner Bros., first building up their television animation unit and later as head of Warner Digital, Sarnoff came from a rich character heritage. As his own children asked when he told them that he was going to work in Culver City, "What characters do they have?" Tim thought for a moment and realized that this was exactly what appealed to him. Here was a company that had the talent and the technology to create just about anything.

So began Imageworks' journey to *Stuart Little.* Sarnoff's personal challenge was to identify a project and

"*Stuart Little was one of my favorite books as a child, mainly because it was an empowerment story. Stuart is three inches tall and every day he goes out into the world, faces daunting obstacles, and somehow comes out okay. I think the story is very cathartic. I always liked the way Stuart solves problems. He's inventive. He has a big heart. He adapts to his environment. I guess I always wanted to be Stuart Little.*"

—DOUGLAS WICK, PRODUCER

make it happen. While Imageworks had a reputation for producing extraordinary digital images, its character animation work, while rewarded with accolades that include two World Animation Celebration Awards, had yet to be tested under the rigors of an operation of the size and scale of *Stuart Little.* That didn't stop Sarnoff from recognizing a great opportunity when he learned of Columbia Pictures' interest in bringing *Stuart Little* to the screen. The magic of *Stuart Little* was clearly dependent upon the character's realism and performance, and Tim was determined to make this dream come true even if no one had yet created a photo-realistic CG (computer graphic) star for a live-action film.

At the same time that artists were sketching and sculpting possible images for Stuart, Richard Kriegler created these Photoshop renderings using the face of a real mouse.

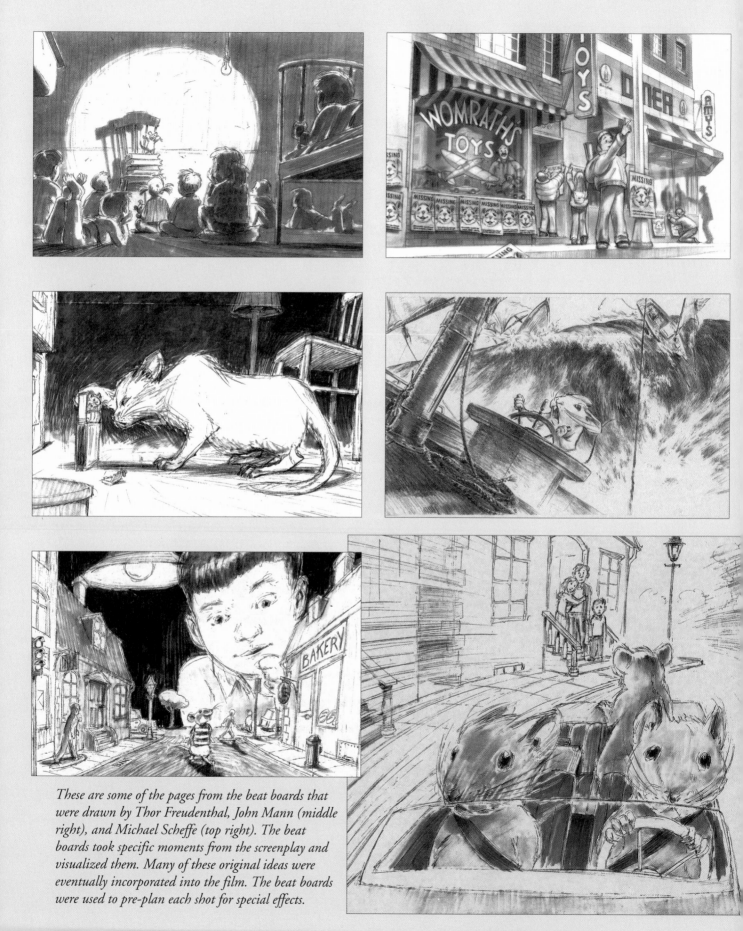

These are some of the pages from the beat boards that were drawn by Thor Freudenthal, John Mann (middle right), and Michael Scheffe (top right). The beat boards took specific moments from the screenplay and visualized them. Many of these original ideas were eventually incorporated into the film. The beat boards were used to pre-plan each shot for special effects.

JASON CLARK ON THE BEAT BOARDS

*B*efore the script was finalized, the purpose of the beat boards was to help conceptualize the film and story as Rob Minkoff and the artists conceived it. Essentially, the beat boards became a snapshot that incorporated the various elements (that is, characters, sets, actions) that we used to estimate the budget and schedule for the movie. Reviewing the beat boards also became the first pass at discussing the interaction of computer graphic images with the live-action environment. For example, the boards showed us where Stuart's fur and clothes mixed with live-action water. This meant we needed to address: How do we get them wet? How do they look wet? How many shots do we need it for? Can we afford several shots? Do we have the schedule to keep Stuart wet for the whole scene or can we only afford to get him wet at the end of the scene?

These discussions allowed the CG team to define what they would need from a 600-plus-shot pipeline and gave them the opportunity to start developing the software. They needed to estimate the number of shots, average complexity of shots, types and average duration of shots, the number and types of costumes, the amount of environmental interactions, and ways to achieve these interactions. One constant question was: Where does the live-action environment end and the CGI environment begin? This went to resolving issues about how much would it cost and how long would it take.

The budget and schedule were fixed yet the script was being rewritten, so we needed to support the artistic team with quick answers to the relative feasibility of what they were thinking. We realized that, in some cases, the vision of the artists may be possible to do once but not in volume. It was easy to put the mice outside the car or inside the car, but to actually see them get in or out of the car was a daunting CG animation problem.

In some cases, it was the live action that was not achievable from the vision of the beat boards, and those discussions in advance of the prep helped minimize painting ourselves in the corner. For example, during the prep of the beat boards for the scene where the Stouts take Stuart away, a beautiful emotional board was drawn showing Stuart and the Stouts in the car, with the Littles on the stoop of their house in the background. The board implied that the camera was moving with Stuart and the Stouts and the Littles are in focus in the receding background. The emotion is with Stuart as he leaves the Littles behind. Fantastic. But the technical team looked at the board and realized it presented a host of problems, such as windscreen reflections, lighting, focus on a moving tiny object, lens height relative to the CGI characters, levelness of the roadway surface, and much more.

Depth of field posed a particularly difficult problem trying to keep such a small object (Stuart in the toy car) and the background (Littles on the stoop) in any relative focus. Did we want to build a CG version of the car in order to control the foreground focus? Would we have other uses for a CG car? There was also a discussion of framing. Could we hold the car in the frame and track with it? Could we get the lens low enough to the ground? Could the camera frame capture the emotion of Stuart (as drawn) and still reveal the Stouts in the foreground and the Littles in the background? Could the car drive on the ground surface without bumping the framing and focus? Would the car need to be rigged on a model mover? Could the camera track with that car for the desired length of the shot? These were only some of the issues that came up based on this simple "beat board" drawing.

We knew that a scene of Stuart going away with the Stouts was going to be in the final script. We knew that he would leave in the toy car with the Stouts, so we knew analyzing this board would go a long way to telling us what we would need to prepare for the live-action filming and the CGI pipeline prior to the completion of the final shooting script.

Tim knew that the talent existed to make this happen. The bigger question was whether or not the technology would support a photo-realistic character. Software became the nexus of the exploration as Chief Technology Officer Lincoln Hu and his scientific team both studied commercially available software and began to write their own computer code for *Stuart Little.*

Meanwhile, Sarnoff authorized Senior Vice President of Animation Production Barry Weiss to form a development team in the digital-character group. Led by Eric Armstrong and several artists, including Thor Freudenthal, a recent top-ranked California Institute of Arts graduate new to Imageworks, animator Todd Wilderman, and modeler Robin Linn, they began regular brainstorming sessions to serve three main purposes: one, to help define the character of Stuart Little; two, to identify the technical challenges of creating the character; and three, to convince the studio that *Stuart Little* could be made in the convincing, photo-realistic manner envisioned by Doug Wick and Columbia Pictures President Amy Pascal.

Out of these early development meetings came the first beat boards (illustrations of major points of the story) and conceptual illustrations, which were convincing enough to lead the studio to establish funding for Imageworks to determine whether or not this collective dream was possible. The project was dubbed SLICE, which stood for Stuart Little Initial Concept Exploration. Artists continued to work with the studio production executives, including Senior Vice President Lori Furie, who was the creative executive supervising the project. At the same time, software teams were busy figuring out how to achieve lifelike fur and cloth. Could off-the-shelf products be used? Or would we have to write our own? After months of testing, it was determined that a combination of the two was the most viable option.

Alias/Wavefront was bringing to market a powerful new suite of software called Maya® that offered versatile animation tools combined with a powerful compositing and effects package. The beauty of the software is its open architecture, which allows for substantial customization. This enabled Imageworks to optimize the software for the specific application of *Stuart Little,* using the best package when appropriate and creating custom software, called "plug ins," to give Stuart his unique form and appearance.

Fortified by the promise that the technology and the desire to make *Stuart Little* was within reach, Columbia elevated *Stuart Little* to the next level, proposing the project to Rob Minkoff to direct.

The success and the attention given to *The Lion King* clearly established Minkoff as a filmmaker of the first order. Truly unique in his experience, Minkoff is one of only a handful of artists to have worked in both live action and animation. These qualifications, combined with an extraordinary sensitivity to character and storytelling, made Minkoff an exciting and compelling choice.

Early concept drawings of Stuart Little by Marty Kline.

With Minkoff onboard, the creative direction came into focus. At Imageworks, Minkoff worked closely with the artists in the digital-character group to define Stuart's personality, behavior, characteristics, and story. They used traditional means, such as paper and pencil and clay sculpture, to help them explore the character. A team room was set up where the movie began to take shape on the walls in the form of beat boards.

While Minkoff and the artists were busy with Stuart, the production management team at Imageworks began organizing the right crew and resources for the project. Most of the basic building blocks for accomplishing *Stuart Little* were already in place. The facility had proved its mettle by successfully running two massive shows, *Contact* and *Starship Troopers,* through the company simultaneously. They had also polished their skills in integrating animation with live action on such projects as *Anaconda* and *Godzilla.* Still, even after these large-scale projects, no one had really built a live-action movie around a CG star who could act and deliver lines.

On the animation and design fronts, Imageworks was operating a concurrent team of digital artists led by Visual Effects Supervisor Jerome Chen, a veteran of *Contact* and *Godzilla.* Chen had carved out a reputation for himself as a superb integrator of live-action and digital elements. Coming from a background of hands-on experience as a digital artist himself, he was the perfect choice to lead the digital team. Jay Redd, another young artist who triumphed with his work on the opening shot of *Contact,* an intricate space fly-through from the earth's orbit to the middle of the universe, was put in charge of exploring the fur and lighting. John McLaughlin, another computer graphics supervisor, helped to develop the digital pipeline. Software issues were being addressed by Amit Agrawal and Chris Russell and their team of software engineers.

"I've got to imagine that it was much the same in 1960 when John F. Kennedy said that by the end of the decade the United States was going to put a man on the moon," recalls Barry Weiss, Senior Vice President of Animation Production for Sony Pictures Imageworks. "I'm sure that while the president-elect was setting his goals, there was a team of engineers at NASA who really didn't know how they were going to accomplish the feat but somehow knew that they would succeed."

The show was beginning to reach critical mass. The studio liked what it saw in the development process. The give-and-take between the artists was positive. The parallel process of developing the technology was reassuring to the artistic side in that it meant that their visions

This screen test featuring a live-action cat and an early digital Stuart helped the animation and visual effects team define its production requirements.

could be brought to the screen effectively. And an eight-minute videotape of the beat board illustrations for the boat-race sequence shown to Columbia Pictures executives enabled the project to move to the next step.

Stuart would have a screen test.

By now, Executive Producer Jason Clark was setting up the show on three, almost four, separate tracks: a live-action first unit, an extensive second unit, a visual effects and animation unit, and a cat unit. If *Stuart Little* was going to succeed, it would do so because of the preparation and organization that went into it. And that, it was proven, was a collective effort on the part of many professionals working together.

In this still-early process, it was clear to Clark, Minkoff, Producer Doug Wick, the studio, and Imageworks that the person who would lead the visual effects team would have to be someone conversant with the entire range of existing visual effects techniques and who would be a willing conspirator in the development of new methods. That combination of existing knowledge and a propensity for invention pointed in one direction—to Academy Award winner John Dykstra. A masterful photographer, a brilliant engineer, an adept director, and a visual stylist, Dykstra was the natural choice.

Dykstra joined the *Stuart Little* team as senior visual effects supervisor and second unit director. In addition to working with the main unit and Imageworks to determine the methods by which each of the more than 650 visual effects shots would be accomplished, Dykstra was responsible for directing a substantial second unit that filmed the cats, an elaborate car-and-cat-chase sequence, the boat race, and the former miniature golf course home of Camille and Reginald Stout.

Animation is as much an art form as it is a tradition, and the truly great animation directors understand how to apply the principles of animation in today's work. Behind every great animated character is a great animation director. Rob Minkoff knew this well, having had the good fortune to enter the business through Cal Arts at a time when great animators like Chuck Jones, Frank and Ollie, and others were still working. With so much of *Stuart Little* to be carried by its animated star, the choice of an animation director was critical to the success of the project. The ideal person would embrace the challenge and would provide the guidance and leadership to keep thirty individuals consistent in creating a uniform character.

Henry F. Anderson III, an Emmy Award winner for *The Last Halloween* and a skilled animation director known for his work at Pacific Data Images (PDI),

Rhythm and Hues, Pixar, and Digital Domain, is one of a handful of true masters of digital-character animation. His Coca-Cola polar bears, for instance, created an international sensation for the soft-drink maker.

Casting an animation director is much like casting an actor, and the moment Rob Minkoff met Henry, he knew he had found the man who would bring Stuart to life. For, ultimately, it is the job of the animation director to create the performance. The relationship established between Minkoff and Anderson was very much that of a director and his star. Rob would discuss performance issues with Henry in exactly the same manner that he would speak with any of the film's live-action stars. In essence, Henry became Stuart personified.

THE SCREEN TEST

A tiny set of clothes designed to illustrate scale, a fluffy white Persian cat, Rob Minkoff, John Dykstra, and a camera crew and hope gathered on a stage at the Imageworks physical production facility to shoot what would be a pivotal moment in the production of *Stuart Little.* If hundreds of shots were to be produced featuring the character of *Stuart Little,* it was clear that an efficient means of producing those shots had to be developed.

Dykstra, Chen, and the animation team devised a shot in which there would be performance, interaction

between the character's hands and fur, interaction between the live-action cat and the CG Stuart, long shots, close-ups, and camera movement. The goal was to determine exactly what it would take in terms of resources—physical, technical, and human—to create the character and integrate him into the live-action world. As the star of the movie, Stuart is in almost every scene, so efficiencies had to be devised. The screen test was meant to determine what it would take to get him into the film—on time and on budget.

The screen test was an amazing experience for the studio and the production team. When viewed today, it looks rough and crude, but it was a milestone achievement. Not only did *Stuart* project a performance that showed promise, but the process of creating the shot clearly identified how to make this movie.

The screen test convinced the studio to green-light the movie. What had been thought of as cinematic impossibility was now a reality.

On his first night home with his adopted family, Stuart is tucked into bed by the Littles. Geena Davis leans over and kisses him good night. To accomplish this, the actress was instructed to kiss the empty space. Later, Stuart would be added to the live-action film. Here is how the scene was shot and how it looked after being worked on by the artists and technicians at Imageworks.

STUART'S 4^1/$_2$-SECOND AUDITION TAPE

*T*he most amazing moment for me in making this movie was the first time we saw a final shot of Stuart on film. Up until then, we were only working with the idea of Stuart and a lot of empty space on film. Then we saw the scene where Geena Davis leans into the frame and kisses Stuart good night. The performance lasted four and a half seconds and it was thrilling.

—JASON CLARK, EXECUTIVE PRODUCER

*W*e were lulled into a false sense of confidence by our first shot of Stuart, the four-and-a-half-second performance of Geena kissing him good night. It worked perfectly but, of course, it turned out to be Stuart's easiest scene. He was sitting in bed. Later in the film, he has to walk, run, and move around, which proved to be much more complicated to pull off.

—JEROME CHEN, VISUAL EFFECTS SUPERVISOR

The Artists

In 1945, artist Garth Williams made the first drawing of Stuart Little. He drew Stuart much the way White had described him, as a tiny guy with mouselike qualities. As befitting the times, Williams's Stuart wore a fedora and dressed in three-piece suits. He was a dapper little character who bore a strong resemblance to his creator, the urbane New Yorker E. B. White. Williams's drawings of a sophisticated Stuart worked for the book because, in the original story, Stuart ages to manhood and leaves home to find his way in the world.

The movie version refocused on a story about a mouse who finds a place in a human family and on the character of Stuart as a child, somewhere between the ages of seven and nine. To look like a kid of the '90s, Stuart needed a radical makeover.

From the very beginning, it was determined that the movie would use state-of-the-art technology and computer animation to create a photo-realistic mouse. The point was to make Stuart look as real as possible so that audiences would think he was actually a mouse who could act. But first, some very important questions needed to be answered: What would he look like? Would he be more mouselike or more like a little boy? How tall would he be? What would his hands look like? Would he walk on all fours or upright? What kind of clothes would he wear?

To visualize the character, director Rob Minkoff and other talented artists began making illustrations and sculptures of Stuart Little. Their job was to create a look for Stuart and to establish specific parameters for the character, which would then be translated by the computer-graphic artists.

Among the first to draw personality studies

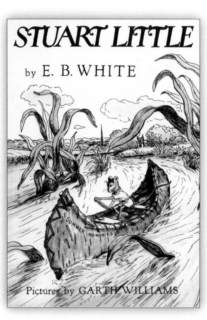

of Stuart were Todd Wilderman and Thor Freudenthal, who created situations for the mouse that helped define his character. So here was Stuart as Edward Scissorhands and Marlon Brando, among many other personas. "We were trying to figure out who Stuart was," explains sculptor Robin Linn, "so we started with who he wasn't. That helped define his personality."

Artists held long discussions about Stuart and, in these meetings, Minkoff contributed rough sketches to show his ideas for the mouse. "First, you look at mice and what they really look like," explains Minkoff, "and then you extract from that a kind of caricature that gives personality to the creation. We needed to find different ways of exaggerating what seems natural about a mouse without falling into the trap of being too cute. A texture and an edge had to remain."

From Rob's sketches, artists expanded on the look of Stuart and tried to find that fine line between having Stuart be lovable but not so sweet that he edges toward a phony sentimentality. "In the film adaptation, Stuart's a very pure character," says Minkoff, "so it was hard to find a handle on how to make him interesting and not totally vanilla."

Many ideas were tried and then discarded. At one point, for example, the artists gave Stuart glasses and imagined him with a British accent. Both characteristics were dropped very early on in the process.

Another early idea was to have other animals in the movie who would interact with Stuart. In a favorite drawing that hangs in many offices at Imageworks, Todd Wilderman drew Stuart in public school with a pig for a classmate. "Ultimately, we eliminated the concept of other animals because it seemed to detract from Stuart's specialness," explains Robin Linn. A decision was made

The original cover and drawing of Stuart Little by Garth Williams from the 1945 book.

that the cats would be the only other animals in the movie and that they would talk, but only to each other and to Stuart. In the end, the mice are the only animals in the movie who talk with humans.

In addition to the more than three hundred sketches and drawings, Stuart was sculpted in clay and plaster by artists Jimmy McPherson, Henry Darnell, Brian Wade, and Robin Linn to give him dimension and visualize his look more closely. "Rob requested as many different ideas as we could put together," recalls Robin Linn. About thirty different sculptures were eventually created, though none of them look exactly like the final Stuart.

The next step was for the artists to create beat boards, or drawings of Stuart in situations that might become part of the story. Creating these free-form explorations is one of the traditional techniques of animation. Artists worked on drawings of Stuart in the orphanage, sailing a boat, talking with his brother, and flying an airplane. Though many of these scenes were never filmed, the boards helped show what the character would look like once he was placed within the framework of the movie.

Once the story was finalized, each scene in the movie was drawn in storyboard format. In every film, storyboards are used to show camera angles and how the director wants each scene to look. For a movie as complex as *Stuart Little*, storyboards are like a bible. Every change in the story or to Stuart's character demanded a detailed storyboard that would be distributed to all the departments involved. The boards were also used to budget the complexities of integrating CGI characters into a live-action environment. Literally thousands of storyboard drawings were made for this movie, right up until the final days of production.

A very early idea was to include other animals in the story who would talk with Stuart. Here Todd Wilderman imagined Stuart in public school with a pig for a classmate. In the end, this idea was abandoned because it seemed to distract from Stuart. While the cats talk to one another and to Stuart, the mice (Stuart and the Stouts) are the only animals in the movie who talk with the humans.

Early concept drawings by Thor Freudenthal and Todd Wilderman imagined Stuart as all the characters he would not be: Edward Scissorhands, Brando, among others. This kind of exercise helped everyone focus on Stuart's personality.

On the Mouse Pad with Stuart: Preproduction and Beyond

The creation of Stuart Little the actor involved four hundred days of labor on the part of 150 artists, animators, and technicians at Sony Pictures Imageworks studios in Culver City, California. "In order to have an extraordinary film, you have to start with the premise that you will do something that you don't know how to do," says Senior Visual Effects Supervisor John Dykstra, explaining the challenge of making Stuart the most lifelike computer-generated character to date.

Following rough sketches drawn by director Rob Minkoff, Imageworks animator Todd Wilderman, storyboard artist Thor Freudenthal, and the many sculptures of Stuart, the visual effects team (helmed by Dykstra, Animation Director Henry Anderson III, and Visual Effects Supervisor Jerome Chen) began working on creating a digital Stuart.

Everyone agreed that as a leading man and the protagonist of the story, Stuart needed to be both lovable and cute, though his "cuteness" was a much-debated point. "We were very careful to stay away from the bad parts of mice that might frighten people or not be so charming and keep the qualities that make mice cute," explains Chen. There were, of course, many different

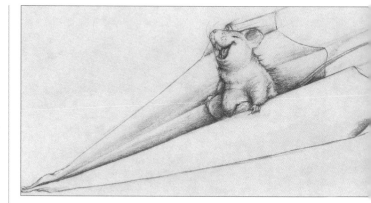

ideas of what constituted "cuteness" in a mouse. "There is no magic button you can press that says, 'Okay, he's cuter now,'" says Chen. "Everyone seemed to have a different idea of what 'cute' meant." Stuart was drawn and then redrawn hundreds of times. Every aspect of his look was painstakingly considered, from the placement of each whisker to the shape of his hands.

"We went through many, many variations on the look of Stuart," says Chen. "But it was very interesting because when we came up with the final image, everyone agreed on it. There was just no doubt in anyone's mind and we were very comfortable showing it to everyone in the studio. Looking back on the earlier versions, we were stunned. How could we ever have thought they were cute? It was a good epiphany—that moment when we were sure we had hit the mark."

While Dykstra and Chen concentrated on Stuart's exterior (his fur and clothing), animation director Henry Anderson III and his team of thirty animators got inside the mouse's head and focused on Stuart's perfor-

Stuart is a mouse who walks on his hind legs. This created many questions for his team of animators. How should he move his legs? How should he hold his hands? After consultations with Dr. Stuart Sumida, a professor of anatomy at Loma Linda University, the team was advised that a mouse would keep his hands up and keep them tightly clasped. Why? Because this is what mice do.

Everyone agreed that Stuart should be "cute" but everyone had a different idea of how exactly "cute" was defined when referring to a mouse. Some early concepts added braces to his teeth and a bravado to his stature to make him more lovable.

mance. With a directive from Minkoff to "figure out who Stuart is," Anderson went back to the E. B. White book. "I really loved Stuart's never-say-die attitude," says Anderson. "I really liked that he was willing to tackle anything. Stuart doesn't see himself as a mouse. He sees himself as just another kid . . . a kid with some of the characteristics of a mouse." To give Stuart a jaunty, bouncy little walk worthy of his optimism, Anderson studied the acting and gestures of silent-film-great Buster Keaton, and with Minkoff videotaped eccentric dancer and comic mime artist Bill Irwin acting out some of Stuart's motions.

Truly the star of the movie, Stuart appears in nearly every scene, altogether some five hundred separate shots, each several seconds long. Every one of Stuart's appearances on-screen is made up of small moments called "shots." "A shot is basically one camera setup in the film," explains Chen. "We use an average shot length of say one hundred fifty frames, which is four or five seconds. Rendering each frame can be very time intensive in terms of computer time."

The animation process began with the live-action film, which was shot over the course of many months. In the film, shots were composed to leave space for Stuart. Dykstra, Chen, Anderson, Visual Effects Plate Photography Supervisor Dave Stump, and a team of matchmovers were on the set making sure that Stuart was lit properly and given correct focus. Also, they collected massive amounts of data concerning technicalities such as camera angles and lighting sources, all of which would be digitally re-created for Stuart's appearance on film.

An early concept drawing of Stuart on a shoe (below) later became the poster image.

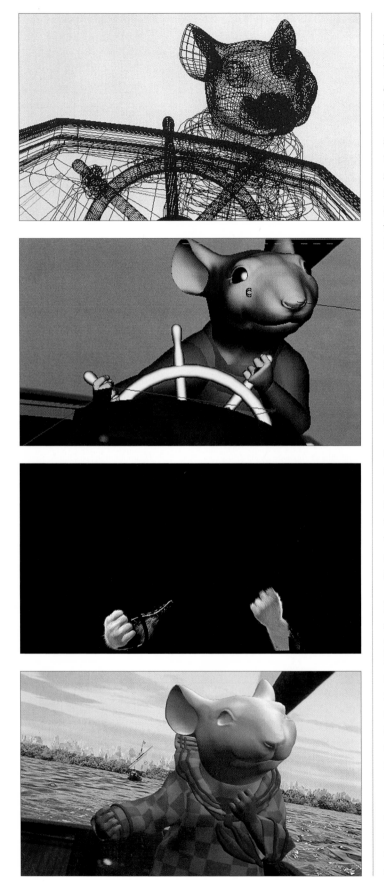

The live-action film was then scanned into the computer so that it would exist in the digital realm, and animators began working on the spaces that had been left blank for Stuart. They re-created the lighting and depth of the camera angles that had existed on the set so that the computer-generated images of Stuart were compatible with his live costars. Then Anderson and his team animated Stuart's movements with a version of Stuart that resembled a plain gray mannequin, without clothes, and was known as "gray mouse." For each scene, the animators produced several "takes," just as would be expected of any human actor. Anderson then conferred with Minkoff in making the final selection of the acting for that shot.

Once a particular gesture was final, Dykstra and Chen's team added the crucial details. "So we have a head, the eyes, the whiskers, different parts of his costume—the tie, the shirt, jacket, pants—the shadows that may be projected on the ground, his reflection," says Chen. "Each of these are rendered separately as individual elements and then combined into what we call a 'composité.' We do this because we can finesse each layer independent of the other." This is where the shots were finished.

"The computer can generate all kinds of different artifacts and they may look weird," says Chen. Digital artists can catch these details and they can make the necessary adjustments to correct such digital imperfections as a poorly rendered shadow or an odd line. When a shot was, in studio lingo, "finaled," the artist working on it was rewarded with a small, round Stuart sticker slapped outside his cubicle. At the end of production, the walls of several workstations were covered with stickers.

Stuart, whose size in the movie is about three inches high, depending on the background he is set against, ended up with the body, hands, and teeth of a seven-year-old boy. Like his brother, he has morning hair when he wakes up. He wears clothes that are right out of the catalog pages of contemporary fashion catalogs. He is as real as the nose on your face. Fifty-five years after he first drew Stuart Little, Garth Williams might recognize the spirit of the character he drew so long ago firmly entrenched in this new Stuart who is, quite literally, a mouse made for the new millennium.

Several stages in the evolution of Stuart Little as he was created on the computer by the Imageworks team. This amazing process is explained in more detail by John Dykstra, Senior Visual Effects Supervisor, on page 118.

THE ILLUSTRATED SCRIPT

SCREENPLAY BY M. NIGHT SHYAMALAN AND GREG BROOKER

BASED ON THE BOOK BY E. B. WHITE

"I think that any family willing to adopt a mouse is a family that I'd like to get to know."
—ROB MINKOFF, DIRECTOR

INT. THE LITTLE'S UPSTAIRS HALLWAY – MORNING
It's early. It's quiet. A cat (Snowbell) is asleep on the floor of the hallway, until . . . a door is flung open so hard it slams against the wall, waking the cat, who shrieks and runs down the stairs.

Bursting through the open doorway is GEORGE LITTLE (eight), full of energy and excitement. He's in his pajamas. He sprints down the hallway and bursts into his parents' room.

INT. MR. AND MRS. LITTLE'S ROOM – CONTINUOUS
George bursts in and jumps in their bed, waking them.

> GEORGE *(excited, jumping on the bed)*
> It's today! It's today! It's today! It's today!

EXT. LITTLE HOUSE – MORNING
The Littles walk to George's school bus.

> MRS. LITTLE
> It's always today, George.

> GEORGE
> I mean this is the day!

> MRS. LITTLE
> That's right.

> GEORGE
> Can't I come?

> MR. LITTLE
> You have to go to school, George.

Geena Davis, Jonathan Lipnicki, and Hugh Laurie as the Little family.

> GEORGE
> Will he be here when I get home?

> MR. LITTLE
> I think so.

The bus arrives.

> GEORGE
> I'm going to play ball with him. I'm going to wrestle with him. I'm going to teach him how to spit.

> MRS. LITTLE
> It's going to be so much fun.

GEENA DAVIS ON HER COSTAR STUART LITTLE

*A*ctually, I had met and worked with Stuart before this movie. We worked together in *A League of Their Own*. He had a very tiny part. It's okay to say "tiny" by the way. People think he's really sensitive about short jokes but, in fact, he's not.

Anyway, he had this tiny part in the movie as a hot-dog vendor, but they had to cut the scene because he could carry only one hot dog at a time and nobody could hear him yelling but he was great. We got to hang out together and get to know each other then. It's really funny and weird that I'd end up playing his mother now.

During rehearsals we had to get over the fact that we'd known each other before, but it happened very naturally. As his mother in this movie, I found myself getting very protective of him off camera. I'd always be watching where they were moving the heavy equipment around Stuart because the bottom line is that he could easily be killed.

MR. LITTLE
For all of us.

George starts to get on the bus. He stops.

GEORGE
How will you know if you're picking the right one?

Mr. and Mrs. Little look at each other.

MR. LITTLE/MRS. LITTLE
I don't know . . . we'll . . .

GEORGE
You'll just know.

MRS. LITTLE
Bye sweetie.

George is on the bus. It pulls away. George sticks his head out the window.

GEORGE
Remember. I want a little brother, not a big brother.

They wave good-bye.

EXT. ORPHANAGE – DAY – ESTABLISHING SHOT

INT. MRS. KEEPER'S OFFICE – MORNING

MRS. KEEPER
We've been through your application. Everything seems to be in order. All that's left is for you to choose one of our hopeful young candidates. Let me just say how happy it makes me seeing a couple such as yourselves choosing to adopt. It's not for everyone, but you seem like the kind of people who have plenty of love to share. So . . . how are you feeling?

MRS. LITTLE
Goodness. We're . . .

MR. LITTLE
. . . tingling.

MRS. LITTLE
. . . with anticipation.

They take each other's hands. A SHRILL BELL RINGS.

MRS. KEEPER
Ah, recess. Time for you to meet them.

Julia Sweeney as Mrs. Keeper.

THE ORPHANAGE

We tried to create a timeless kind of New York; a fairy tale New York with enough reality so that you knew it was Manhattan, but without some of the harsher aspects such as graffiti and dirt.

We treated the orphanage set as one zone, as a world without color. Everything here from the floors to the uniforms to the mural on the wall was either black or blue or a nondescriptive beige-yellow, the color of concrete.

—BILL BRZESKI, PRODUCTION DESIGNER

We hear the sounds of bouncy, excited children bursting out of classrooms.

MRS. KEEPER *(cont'd)*
Feel free to walk around. They're quite used to having strangers here.

MR. AND MRS. LITTLE
Thank you.

Mr. and Mrs. Little exit. Mrs. Keeper shuts the door.

MRS. KEEPER
Ah. . . . Lovely people.

INT. ORPHANAGE PLAYGROUND – CONTINUING
A long, thin, wooden-floored playground with tetherball poles, and basketball hoops . . . and a hundred yelling KIDS. Huge overhead windows throw shafts of sunlight. WE FOLLOW Mr. and Mrs. Little walking past a line of bunk beds. They observe kids at play: Tag. Sock-ball. Hop-Scotch. And all of it punctuated by laughter. You'd never know these children were orphans.

Mrs. Little stares at all these hopeful faces, visibly moved. Mr. Little takes her hand. Then:

The Littles sit down on a bench.

The orphanage set, from early concept drawings to the way it looks at filming.

MRS. LITTLE
Oh, Frederick, look at them. How could we possibly . . .

MR. LITTLE
Choose . . . I know. They all seem so . . .

MRS. LITTLE
. . . wonderful.

VOICE (O.S.)
You know what I was thinking? I was thinking how wonderful it is that you both know what the other one is going to say, before you even say it.
(beat)
Not that it's any of my business.

A MOUSE – STANDING RIGHT BETWEEN THEM
Three inches tall, wearing an orphanage uniform with a miniature BOOK (*Little Women*) in his hands. This is STUART.

MR. LITTLE
Yes, well that happens when you've been together as long as we have . . .

MRS. LITTLE
. . . from being a family.

STUART
Family . . . Wow! Well, for family you've certainly come to the right place. I think we can find just what you're looking for. You know, if you want

a girl . . .
(pointing)
Susan can read French. And Edith over there can
tap dance while blowing bubbles . . .

A little girl, Edith tap dances while blowing a bubble.

STUART *(cont'd)*
Or maybe you wanted a boy?

Mr. and Mrs. Little take a moment to make eye contact
and absorb this event.

MR. LITTLE
Actually, I think we were leaning toward a boy.

STUART
Well, in that case . . . Benny can do handstands.
And Andy can run a hundred yards faster than you
can say "Ready, Set, Go!"

A little boy, Andy, takes off running.

STUART *(cont'd)*
Andy, no . . . I . . . uh.

MRS. LITTLE
You certainly know a lot about everyone, don't you.

STUART
Well, that's what happens when you've been here as
long as I have. I mean, let's face it. Not everyone
wants to adopt someone like me.

*Thor Freudenthal's early drawing of Mr. and Mrs. Little
meeting Stuart for the first time at the orphanage.*

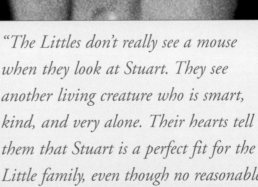

"*The Littles don't really see a mouse when they look at Stuart. They see another living creature who is smart, kind, and very alone. Their hearts tell them that Stuart is a perfect fit for the Little family, even though no reasonable person could possibly agree.*"

—DOUGLAS WICK, PRODUCER

"The fact that Stuart dresses in clothing distinguishes him from other mice who tend not to wear clothes."
—ROB MINKOFF, DIRECTOR

He puts his book back in a bookshelf. The Littles study him . . . then return their collective gaze to this room full of children.

STUART (cont'd)
You shouldn't worry about choosing. It happens the same way every time. First you won't know what to do. You'll be a little bit scared. Then you'll meet one of them. Talk to him. And somehow . . . you'll just know.

Mr. Little eyes his wife. The sound of all that laughter fills the air. Stuart leans on globe and stumbles.

CUT TO:
INT. OFFICE – DAY
MRS. KEEPER looks across the table, utterly unnerved.

MRS. KEEPER (uncomfortably)
Are you quite certain that you're prepared to handle his . . . uniqueness?

MR. LITTLE
Oh my yes. Yes, his uniqueness is a perfect fit for the Little family.

MRS. LITTLE
Perfect.

MRS. KEEPER
Mr. and Mrs. Little, we try to discourage couples from adopting children outside their own . . . species. It rarely works out.

MRS. LITTLE
Well, it will in this case.

CUT TO:
INT. OFFICE – DAY
CLOSE on a paper being rolled into a typewriter.

The top of the paper reads, "Adoption Form." The paper is scrolled to the line marked, "New name." The letters come on in a staccato burst.

"S-T-U-A-R-T L-I-T-T-L-E"

CUT TO:

EXT. ORPHANAGE – AFTERNOON

The children explode out the front doors of the orphanage onto the street, shouting and waving at the bright yellow checker cab carrying Stuart and the Littles.

> KIDS
> BYE, STUART! GOOD LUCK! SEE YA ROUND TOWN!

He waves. The cab disappears down the road . . . heading toward the Manhattan skyline.

CUT TO:

EXT. LITTLE HOUSE – DAY

We OPEN ON the tops of two tall buildings separated by a relatively short space. WE PAN DOWN as we hear:

> MR. LITTLE (O.S.)
> Well, Stuart, here we are . . . the family home. They say every Little in the world knows how to find this house, even if they've never been here before.

WE REVEAL the family brownstone occupying the space between the two tall buildings.

INT. LITTLE HOME – ENTRY

The door opens and Stuart stands in the doorway with the Littles. He looks around, speechless. The place is timeless, lovely.

> MRS. LITTLE
> Just something inside them.

The enchanting home reflects in Stuart's wide eyes . . .

MECHANICAL EFFECTS

*I*n addition to the CGI (Computer Graphics Imaging) effects in this movie, many mechanical effects were also needed. For example, when we first meet Stuart, he is holding a small-sized copy of *Little Women* in his hands. While talking to the Littles, he takes his tiny book and puts it on the shelf alongside other books. Mechanical effects supervisor Eric Allard and special effects technician Bruce Hayes rigged a mechanism inside of the books to make them move apart when Stuart puts his book between them. Stuart's book was a CGI special effect but he moves the live-action books, then lets go of them and the books stop where they should stop. For many of the computer-generated special effects, there was a corresponding mechanical effect that had to first be filmed.

—ERIC ALLARD
MECHANICAL EFFECTS SUPERVISOR

Above left: Bruce Hayes and Eric Allard working on the books in Stuart's bookcase. Below: The scene where the Littles' taxi pulls away from the orphanage was shot from atop an eighty-foot scaffolding.

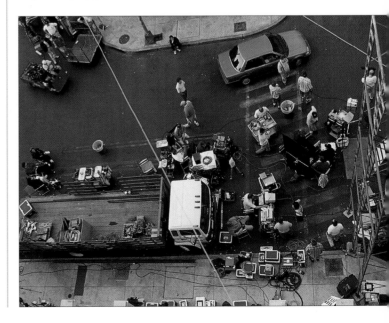

STUART *(whispers)*
Something inside.

MR. LITTLE
So, would you like a tour?

STUART
I don't have any money.

CUT TO:

INT. HALL – DAY

Stuart stands on the mail table and looks at the many photographs that don the walls. Mrs. Little narrates:

MRS. LITTLE
That's Uncle Crenshaw, Cousin Edgar, Grandpa Spencer. That's Aunt Beatrice . . .
(stops)
. . . and that's George. Your brother.

Stuart stops, and stares at the framed picture: It's a school portrait.

STUART
Look, he's already happy to see me.

Not only did production designer Bill Brzeski create amazing human-sized sets, but also, because the star was only three inches tall, he had to pay close attention to floor space and the foreground and background space. He carefully selected floor patterns and moldings to ensure that they would be visually pleasing when blown up on the movie screen. Below: Art director Phil Toolin and production designer Bill Brzeski.

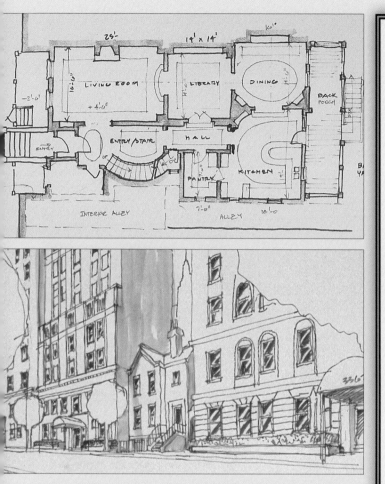

Above: The evolution of the Little house, in sketches and blueprints. Below: Historical Stage 15, where film classics such as The Wizard of Oz *were shot, became the home for the movie's re-created section of New York City's Fifth Avenue. A real tar street was poured, complete with street grades, manholes, and cracked sidewalks.*

THE LITTLE HOUSE

"They say every Little in the world knows how to find this house, even if they've never been here before."
—MR. LITTLE

The Littles are an ancient New York family. Generations ago, probably in the early 1800s, the family bought that house on Fifth Avenue. By the turn of the century, other buildings started going up around them, but the family held out and refused to move. (This idea was taken from an actual house on Fifth Avenue.) The Little house tells us that the Littles believe in tradition and family.

It's a very special house where everyone wants to live. When you walk inside, you know you're surrounded by gentle people. The Littles have good taste and they read good books. The décor has a timeless quality; not so conservative or traditional that it feels dated, yet not so fantastic that it dominates the scenes. The house is filled with contemporary stuff you'd find in most houses: an Apple computer, CDs and stereo, a TV in the kitchen, and such.

When we decorate a house for a set, we make up a personal background for the occupants. If it's a house for a stockbroker, for example, we know to include a copy of the *Wall Street Journal.* For *Stuart Little*, we imagined that Mrs. Little was a music teacher. (Early in production there was a scene in the music room where she plays the piano with Stuart, but that was cut from the movie.) Mr. Little, we believed, was a museum curator, and we placed lots of little collections of things around the house. Basically, we made him like a big version of George.

I am very proud of this movie. Most movies fall short of the goals you set, but with *Stuart Little* we really achieved everything we set out to accomplish.

—BILL BRZESKI, PRODUCTION DESIGNER

Above (inset): Thor Freudenthal's early drawing of Snowbell's first encounter with Stuart.

MR. LITTLE
Well, that's just about everybody. Except for . . .

But just then:

OUT OF NOWHERE – A BLUR
It's Snowbell, who rockets around a corner, barreling straight at Stuart.

Before he has time to think, Stuart is sucked into Snowbell's mouth. Gone, just like that. The Littles gasp.

MRS. LITTLE
Snowbell! Drop him right now!

MR. LITTLE
You spit Stuart out this instant, Snowbell! Spit him right out!

Snowbell studies them, confused as hell; where's my pat on the head? But when Mr. Little takes a menacing step in Snowbell's direction, the cat spits Stuart out quickly.

Stuart drops to the ground, slimy and wet, his suit ruined.

MRS. LITTLE
Stuart, are you all right?

STUART
Wait?!

Stuart checks himself, his limbs to see if they're all there. He finds his tail.

> STUART *(cont'd)*
> I'm fine!

> MR. LITTLE
> You must never harm Stuart, do you understand?

> MRS. LITTLE
> Never! Or out you'll go, Mister Snow.

> MR. LITTLE
> Stuart is one of the family now. We do not eat family members.

Snowbell stares, unable to process this information.

INT. LITTLE ENTRANCE HALL – DAY

George rushes in.

> GEORGE
> Where is he?

> MRS. LITTLE
> He's here. Stuart, this is George. George, this is Stuart . . . your new brother.

Stuart stands proudly, excited. George stares at Stuart — then at his parents.

> GEORGE *(calmly)*
> No really.

> MR. LITTLE
> Really, George. This is your new brother.

Stuart hurriedly wipes his hand clean, extending it for a nice-to-meet-you shake . . . but George just stares.

> GEORGE
> You look somewhat like a mouse.

> STUART
> I am . . . somewhat like a mouse.

> GEORGE
> I see . . . *(a beat)* I have to go . . .

Snowbell meows.

> GEORGE *(cont'd)* *(he picks up Snowbell)*
> Come on, Snowbell. Let's go downstairs.

An upset George opens the door to the basement — Snowbell is right on his heels. Before the cat disappears he looks back at the Littles . . . is that a smile?

The door shuts, and we hear the unmistakable sound of a LOCK being thrown.

Stuart lowers his hand. The Littles smile thinly. There's a silent moment.

> STUART
> Is it just me or did he seem a little disappointed?

> MRS. LITTLE
> Well, he's always a little tired after school.

> MR. LITTLE
> He perks up around dinnertime.

> MRS. LITTLE *(nods)*
> Hmmm.

INT. DINING ROOM – NIGHT
The Littles are eating dinner. It's tense. George has definitely not perked up.

MR. LITTLE
Meat loaf is delicious, dear.

MRS. LITTLE
Cajun. Shall we get to know each other a little?
George, don't you have anything you want to ask
Stuart?

STUART
Sure, George, go ahead. I'm an open book. Ask me
anything. The first thing that pops into your head.

GEORGE *(to Stuart)*
Can you pass the gravy?

For Stuart this would be impossible and George
knows it.

INT. LITTLE HOME – STUART'S BEDROOM – NIGHT

MRS. LITTLE
Your new bedroom, Stuart.

MR. LITTLE
We hope you like it.

REVEAL Stuart in bed, almost lost amid the vastness of
his new bed.

STUART
It sure is roomy.

Stuart looks around the room — chairs and dressers
and toy chests, all human-sized.

Mrs. Little leans in, kisses his forehead.

STUART *(cont'd)*
Good night, Mom. Good night . . . Dad.

MR. LITTLE
Good night . . . Son.

They start to leave.

MRS. LITTLE
Good night, sweetie.

Out goes the light.

They exit. Stuart is very happy.

He stares at the ceiling. His new room. His eyes close.

INT. STUART'S BEDROOM – NIGHT
Stuart is tucked into bed. A crack of light appears . . .
and Snowbell creeps in. He jumps on the bed — and
Stuart's eyes open. A long . . . silent moment between
them. Until —

STUART
Nice Kitty. Nice Kitty. Pretty Kitty.

SNOWBELL
Are you COZY????

STUART
Yes. Thanks— I'm quite comfort—

SNOWBELL *(cutting off Stuart)*
'Cause all I've got to sleep on is a rag in the corner
you little RAT!

STUART
You seem tense.

SNOWBELL
Tense! I am way past tense!

STUART
Well, maybe I can help. What do you like? Can I scratch your ears? I could rub your tummy.

Stuart tries to pet Snowbell.

SNOWBELL
How'd you like to rub it from the inside, mouseboy?

Stuart removes his hand.

STUART
Sorry, I'm a little confused. I thought that's what you do with a pet.

Snowbell backs Stuart to the foot of the bed.

SNOWBELL
A PET?! I'm not your pet. I'm a CAT . . . you're a MOUSE . . . you should be living in a hole! This is my family.

Above and left: Little house interiors. Production designer Bill Brzeski and staff assembled a 105-page style guide of sketches and palettes for determining how things would exist in Stuart's world. Everything in the house— hardware, cabinetry, even the windows—was made from scratch.

DECORATING THE LITTLE HOUSE

*E*verything inside the house was done in very broad strokes, using primary colors and strong graphics. I was influenced by the color patterns of Edward Hopper, who works with very simple color patterns. To combine the idea of reality and fairy tale, I wanted to emphasize an almost childlike use of color.

Adults are generally afraid to get involved with color; they paint their houses neutral tones like white or beige. Few people will paint a room bright red or green. Children, however, will crayon with bright colors because color is pure emotion. I tried to bring kids into the movie by using bright colors throughout the Little house. So one room is green, another gold, and so forth. The only color missing from the house is blue because that was the color of the orphanage.

—BILL BRZESKI, PRODUCTION DESIGNER

> *"When I was a kid, I spent a lot of time wondering what it would be like if the cat could talk or if the dog could say something or if my dolls were ever going to come to life. I was always expecting that when I turned my back, something like that would happen. I think it's a universal thing that people expect animals to know a lot more than the animals do."*
>
> —GEENA DAVIS

STUART
C-can't we share them?

SNOWBELL
Read my furry, pink lips . . . NO!

Snowbell hops off the bed. He jumps onto the windowsill — and nervously looks around.

SNOWBELL (cont'd)
And stay away from the windows — if the other cats find out about this, I'm ruined.

He jumps away.

EXT. LITTLE HOME – MORNING – ESTABLISHING

INT. UPSTAIRS HALLWAY

Beat board by Michael Scheffe.

Mrs. Little is carrying a laundry basket.

MRS. LITTLE
George, time to get up.

GEORGE (sleepily)
Okay, Mom.

MRS. LITTLE
Stuart, you too.

STUART (sleepily)
Okay, Mom.

She goes downstairs.

INT. HALLWAY – CONTINUING
George, in pajamas, sleepily leaves his room and crosses to the bathroom. He has "morning hair."

A moment later, Stuart, in pajamas that match George's leaves his room and sleepily crosses to the bathroom. Stuart, also, has "morning hair."

INT. GEORGE'S BATHROOM – SAME
George is at the sink, eyeing himself in the mirror. He doesn't notice as STUART ENTERS. Instead he just opens a bottle of mouthwash, and begins to gargle.

Stuart has a tiny table of his own in here, inches high — for his toiletries. He opens a mini-bottle of mouthwash, and gargles as well.

George rinses into the sink. Stuart rinses into a mini-wastepaper basket (a Dixie cup).

George combs his hair. Stuart does the same.

INT. LAUNDRY ROOM

MRS. LITTLE
George, I'm trying to get the laundry started.

INT. GEORGE'S BATHROOM – SAME
George reacts, slightly put upon.

GEORGE (aloud)
Okay.

He pops his pajama top off, and drops it to the floor. *It lands right on top of Stuart*, obscuring him completely.

STUART (muffled)
Hey!

Then George drifts out, until he hears:

INT. LAUNDRY ROOM

MRS. LITTLE
Into the laundry chute, please!

INT. GEORGE'S BATHROOM – SAME
George pops back into the bathroom.

GEORGE
Okay . . .

George scoops the pajamas up from the floor.

INT. LAUNDRY CHUTE – CONTINUING
George opens the chute and dumps the p.j.'s down —
the clothes fall toward camera. Stuart yelps.

INT. LITTLE HOME – LAUNDRY ROOM - SAME
Mrs. Little stands by a front-loading WASHER. She
hears the THUMP of the clothes landing at the bottom
of the chute. (But she doesn't hear the faint "Ouch!")

MRS. LITTLE *(aloud)*
Thank you!

She grabs the clothes and tosses them into the washer.
Then she shuts it, and hits "ON." All we hear is:

STUART (O.S.)
Oh dear . . .

"When we first brought the cats onto the set to meet Stuart, well, he was a little reluctant, understandably, being a mouse and knowing the reputation that some of the cats had before coming here. They'd all played some pretty mean cats in other films. So that first day was a little uneasy for everyone concerned. The whole studio was worried that something would happen. The insurance company was there, of course. Everyone was a little nervous. Here's eight cats and in comes this little mouse in his business suit, ready to say hi and get to work."
—BOONE NARR,
ANIMAL STUNT COORDINATOR

Todd Wilderman's illustration of an early idea that was probably inspired by the E. B. White book. In the process of making the film, the character of George underwent many changes. At first, according to Rob Minkoff, "George was a twelve-year-old boy and sort of troubled." In the end, though, George became a much younger boy and not at all as mean as Wilderman drew him here.

INT. WASHING MACHINE – CONTINUING

Water begins to fill the machine. Stuart starts banging on the glass window of the machine.

> STUART (CONT'D)
> Mom! Mom! Hello, Mom. It's Stuart. I'm in the washing machine! Mom!

INT. LAUNDRY ROOM – CONTINUING

Mrs. Little doesn't hear him; she's too busy folding the clothes that just came from the dryer. Then, at last, she does hear his BANGING. But:

And she heads out of the laundry room, thinking there's someone at the front door. More water enters the washer . . .

> STUART
> Where're you goin'?!

CUT TO:

INT. LITTLE HOME – FRONT DOOR – CONTINUING
Mrs. Little opens the front door, but no one's there.

> MRS. LITTLE
> That's odd . . .

MR. LITTLE
What is?

MRS. LITTLE
Well, I thought someone was at the door.

MR. LITTLE
You look beautiful, dear.

MRS. LITTLE
Honey, should we talk to George before you go?

MR. LITTLE
About what?

MRS. LITTLE
About Stuart. He hasn't exactly embraced the situation.

MR. LITTLE
Maybe we didn't prepare George well enough ahead of time.

MRS. LITTLE
Not prepare him? We discussed it for months.

MR. LITTLE
Yes, but think back. In our conversations with

"We wanted Stuart to be about family. We wanted the true mayhem of real siblings."
—DOUGLAS WICK, PRODUCER

George we may have given him the distinct impression that we were going to adopt a human being.

MRS. LITTLE *(thinking)*
Oh. You might be right.

INT. LAUNDRY ROOM – CONTINUING
Stuart is banging around inside the washing machine.

Snowbell enters. Stuart can see the cat's face, distorted by the convex curve of the washer window.

STUART
Snowbell! Snowbell, It's Stuart! I'm in here. I'm in the washer. Can you help me? Can you turn this thing off?

SNOWBELL
Why would I turn it off? It's my favorite show.

The cat turns and starts to walk toward the door.

STUART
Ha! That's funny. That's funny, Snowbell. Snowbell, come back! Please!

SNOWBELL
Talk to the butt.

STUART
Snowbell, where're you going?

SNOWBELL
Oh, I've got to stare at traffic, yawn, lick myself . . . and believe me, that can take hours if you do it right. Ciao.

INT. FRONT DOOR

MR. LITTLE
Are you sure that *Stuart* is happy here?

MRS. LITTLE
Oh, he's having the time of his life.

INT. WASHING MACHINE – CONTINUING
Water fills the machine.

STUART (O.S.)
Help! Somebody! Please help me!

INT. FRONT DOOR – CONTINUING
Mr. and Mrs. Little KISS and he exits.

INSIDE THE WASHING MACHINE

Because of Stuart's size, we treated the washing machine as a set," says mechanical effects supervisor Eric Allard. The set on the live-action shoot had removable sides. Waterproof cables were wired into the clothes to make them appear to be floating in soap suds. A dump tank held the water in position until Geena Davis opened the door.

This shot inside the washing machine includes a myriad of CG enhancements, such as wet and messy clumping fur, CG water with tiny CG splashes, interaction between the CG water and Stuart's tail, and reflections in the glass door of the machine—all of which had to be designed to fully integrate Stuart into the action.

Storyboards *(right)* drawn by Thor Freudenthal, dated 5/26/98 and entitled "Stuart in Washing Machine," follow the sequence where Stuart is inadvertently tossed in with the morning laundry. Pencil notes on the right side of the drawings were made by Senior Visual Effects Supervisor John Dykstra and indicate what effect each shot required, including mechanical effects, CGI, or live action. Notes indicate who is dry and what is wet because such details affected how Stuart's fur would be programmed. In some scenes, Stuart shakes off water and his fur goes from wet to dry. In other shots, he and his fur are tossing about in the water. Every such change required an enormous amount of preparation.

WM/ VFX 12C

LIVE PLATE
MATCH CLOTH
DISPLACEMENT
CG STUART
M.C.

WM/ VFX 12D

LIVE PLATE
MATCH CLOTH
DISPLACE
CG STUART
M.C.

MOM! MOM! I SEEM TO BE
TRAPPED IN THE MAYTAG!

WM/ VFX 12E

INT. LAUNDRY ROOM – CONTINUING

HER POV – THE WASHER
Stuart is pressed up against the washer-window, water and suds surrounding him.

> MRS. LITTLE
> Hi, Stuart.
> *(then)*
> Stuart!!

> STUART *(under water)*
> Mom!

Laundry goes flying.

> MRS. LITTLE
> Oh!

She throws open the washer door — sending water, suds, and a thoroughly soaked Stuart onto the Laundry Room floor . . . She gasps.

He slides across the floor then comes to a stop, coughing.

Dabney Coleman as Dr. Beechwood.

> MRS. LITTLE *(cont'd)*
> Stuart, are you all right?

He coughs again, then sits up. She's too terrified to move.

> STUART
> I'm . . . I'm okay, Mom.

But just as she sighs with relief . . . he passes out.

CUT TO:

INT. STUART'S BEDROOM – NIGHT
Stuart sleeps, we hear a little cough, while DR. BEECHWOOD (55, kind), packs up his medical bag.

And Mr. and Mrs. Little watch from the hall, sick with worry.

Stuart coughs and sneezes.

> MRS. LITTLE
> Is he going to be all right?

DR. BEECHWOOD
A lad that size, swallowing all that detergent . . . amazingly I think he's going to be fine. Also, he's very clean.

INT. LITTLE HOME – HALLWAY – CONTINUING
Beechwood joins the Littles outside Stuart's room.

MRS. LITTLE
This is all my fault. It's all my fault . . .

DR. BEECHWOOD
Well this type of thing was bound to happen.

MR. LITTLE
Maybe he should wear a little bell, so we'll always know where he is.

DR. BEECHWOOD
No . . . It's not that simple. Stuart is a . . . I mean he'll *always* be a . . . And this home. It has human-size doors and human-size windows . . . human-size appliances.
(they nod)
I'm not saying it can't work. I'm just saying there might be some . . . difficulties.

MRS. LITTLE
Oh, well, we don't mind difficulties.

MR. LITTLE
No . . . no . . . no . . . Not at all.

DR. BEECHWOOD
I hope you don't think I'm being rude . . . But you're not the ones it's going to be difficult on.

They ponder that.

MRS. LITTLE *(to Dr.)*
Dr., is there anything else we should do for Stuart?

DR. BEECHWOOD
Well, when you're doing your laundry, just check and make sure it's not moving. My bill.

The doctor was delighted with Stuart and said that it was very unusual for an American family to have a mouse.
—E. B. WHITE, *STUART LITTLE*, 1945

SNOWBELL

Snowbell has an identity crisis because Stuart is adopted and treated like a child. Snowbell feels he's being pushed out of the family by a rodent and that's got to hurt when you're a cat.

—ROB MINKOFF, DIRECTOR

Early concept drawing of Snowbell, with the outline of a bell implanted on his chest, drawn by Todd Wilderman.

He presents them with a bill and leaves.

EXT. DEPARTMENT STORE – DAY – ESTABLISHING
The Littles exit a taxi and walk up to the front door.

MR. LITTLE
Come on, George.

George runs to a window display. Mr. Little follows him.

George stares at the sailboat. Mr. Little has an agenda here, but he's not sure how to approach it . . .

MR. LITTLE
So, George . . . I wanted to talk to you about Stuart. I just want you to know if you and he were to spend some real time together, you know, brother time . . .

STUART'S EARLY CHILDHOOD

*A*s the Animation Supervisor, I led the team of animators who were responsible for Stuart's performance. Obviously, we started with the script, but Rob Minkoff and I had many, many conversations that allowed us to go beyond the words . . . to what was really inside Stuart as a unique personality. We were looking for mannerisms and characteristics that would give dimension to his character.

Both the script and the book portray Stuart as a pretty optimistic guy. He's quite childlike but has a broad range of emotions. Like a child, he can be a bit melodramatic at times. When he's happy, he's very, very happy, and when something is troubling him, he gets really down. Working with that contrast helps us to create a more interesting character.

He's a complicated little guy. He really cares about other people, even if they don't belong to his own species. He's very conscientious about fitting into his new family. He's not there to take advantage of them. He wants to feel welcome but he doesn't want the relationship to be one-sided. Since it's a new thing for him, he is still learning what it means to be part of a family.

He didn't have an easy childhood, losing his parents in a tragic soup can accident when he was quite young. From what I learned while researching the movie, Stuart's real parents were Russian intellectuals who emigrated to America quite by accident. Stuart's father was a leading voice in the persecuted rodent avant garde, forced into exile when a volume of his poetry, *All the Same Under the Fur,* was banned. He and Stuart's mother were exiled to a warehouse where their crate was thrown into a larger crate and sealed. They arrived in America without being able to speak any English. Fortunately, the work of Stuart's father was well known over here, and with the help of friends, both of Stuart's parents found teaching positions at New York University. All was going pretty well until the unfortunate incident in the grocery store.

Stuart had a hard time of it before the Littles came into his life, both emotionally and physically. It was difficult growing up in an orphanage, being the only mouse among all the children. Everything there was scaled for the larger, human-size kids. He was probably underfoot quite a lot and had to find his own way. Always very observant, a trait he probably inherited from his father, Stuart was aware of everything going on around him. And he had to get used to a constant sense of loss as friends came into his life, formed close bonds with him, were adopted, and moved away.

Stuart was a quick learner in school and managed to make his own way in the orphanage. The teachers came to rely on him, and he even stood in once as a substitute when the teacher was out of the classroom. Though he had always dreamed of being adopted, Stuart had almost given up hope. A very tiny voice inside him kept alive the dream that one day he would have a family of his own and that his fairy tale would come true.

—HENRY ANDERSON III
ANIMATION SUPERVISOR

Animation Supervisor Henry Anderson III discusses Stuart's performance with Vladimir Todorov, one of the team of computer animators at Imageworks. During production, Henry would visit the workstations of his animation team several times a day, sometimes on an hourly basis.

GEORGE
Look at that one!

MR. LITTLE
Yeah, well. It's big.

GEORGE
Why did Anton have to get it.

MR. LITTLE
Oh come on, George. You have a boat, a beautiful one.

GEORGE
It's not finished.

MR. LITTLE
Don't you want to race your boat, George?

GEORGE
I'm not so good at the racing part.

MR. LITTLE
So what? You'll practice. It doesn't matter about winning. You try like heck and you have fun.

GEORGE
Is it fun to finish last?

INT. DEPARTMENT STORE – SAME
CLOSE ON Mrs. Little thoughtfully examining something OFF CAMERA.

MRS. LITTLE
Something formal I should think. I'm not sure of the fabric but it should breathe. He does have a tendency to burrow and climb and generally scurry about.

CLOSE ON A HAND holding a very tiny, very loud men's outfit.

CAMERA PULLS BACK revealing that a SALESMAN is displaying the suit to Stuart, who stands on a countertop. We're in the toy department.

SALESMAN
Well, I think we have just the thing that suits your particular needs.

He ducks behind the counter and pops back with a succession of Ben dolls which he swiftly places around Stuart.

SALESMAN (cont'd)
Here we have . . . Barbados Ben . . . Chef Ben . . .

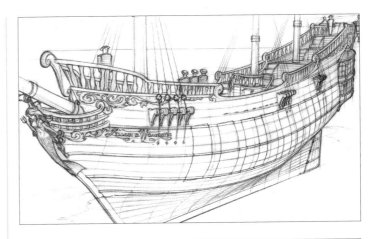

Detailed early drawings of the Lillian B. Womrath, *the nemesis ship to George's* Wasp, *drawn by Michael Scheffe. The final* Womrath *sported huge black sails, giving it a much more menacing appearance than in these drawings.*

"We wanted to completely control the look of the costumes so we made everyone's clothes. Nothing was shopped. We made all the shirts, pants, suits, skirts, and so forth. We made all the clothes for the Little family. In this way, we could also control the color palette. We used colors from the 1940s, the color of the tiles they used in the bathrooms and on wallpapers and such."

—JOSEPH PORRO, COSTUME DESIGNER

Lumberjack Ben . . . Gladiator Ben . . . And, of course, Polo Ben.

Soon Stuart is surrounded.

> MRS. LITTLE
> Yes. Does Ben always dress like this?
>
> SALESMAN
> No, no, no, Madam, there are many moods of Ben and it all depends on the occasion.
>
> MRS. LITTLE
> Well, what if the occasion were a simple family party?
>
> SALESMAN
> I think I have just the thing.

INT. TOY DEPARTMENT- MOMENTS LATER
Mr. Little and George enter the toy department.

> MR. LITTLE
> There they are.

George veers off to check out some toys. Mr. Little joins Mrs. Little.

> MRS. LITTLE *(to Mr. Little)*
> George?
>
> MR. LITTLE
> Hm.
> *(re: Stuart)*
> Shopping?

> MRS. LITTLE
> Hm.

Mrs. Little leans down to the countertop where a tiny, curtained dressing room has been set up.

> MRS. LITTLE
> Stuart, everything all right in there?
>
> STUART (O.S) (behind curtain)
> Don't come in!

Mrs. Little straightens back up, looks over at George, whispers to Mr. Little.

> SALESMAN *(mouthing)*
> Shy.
>
> MR. LITTLE
> The a . . .
>
> MRS. LITTLE
> Ben.

Suddenly, the dressing room curtain opens with a flourish. Stuart saunters out in a CONSERVATIVE SUIT AND BOW TIE like a runway model, but struggles to get into the suit jacket (the Bill Irwin routine). The more he struggles, the more tangled he becomes. He gets it on backward, like a straightjacket. Finally, with a quick spin, he gets the coat on the right way.

> STUART *(clears throat)*
> How do I look?

Early beat board drawing by Eric Armstrong illustrating the scene where Mrs. Little takes Stuart shopping for doll clothes.

STUART'S WARDROBE

As would befit a star of Stuart's stature, costume designer Joseph Porro designed five outfits for Stuart, including his trademark one-button jacket, which was the brainchild of director Rob Minkoff. "I think Stuart seems like a proper kind of character. A little more old school," he says. Indeed, the technician who digitally constructed Stuart's clothing took an old-fashioned approach and studied tailoring to better understand how to create his wardrobe. Animators took sewing classes to learn how to construct and sew fabrics to produce the most realistic effect possible.

The biggest challenge for John Dykstra and Jerome Chen turned out to be getting the drape of Stuart's doll-size clothing and the realistic furriness of his little head rendered satisfactorily.

Due to their impossibly small size, dolls' clothes are often very stiff, but Minkoff wanted Stuart's clothing to flow and his fur to move in the breeze and flatten in the water. Using as their basis Alias/Wavefront's Maya, a software package increasingly used by professional digital-character animators and computer graphics artists, software engineers at Imageworks created custom programs to make Stuart truly furry and to ensure that his outfits were fluid enough to flap in the wind.

"We spent over a year figuring out how the cloth would move on Stuart's body when he runs," explains visual effects supervisor Jerome Chen. "In other words, we made the cloth *follow* the character's performance. For the cloth, we used the cloth plug-in program created by Alias/Wavefront for its Maya software. It performed great after we got together with Alias/Wavefront and worked on the software to solve the scale problems." The realism far surpasses computer-generated clothing on characters of the past.

Four original drawings by costume designer Joseph Porro showing some early ideas for Stuart's wardrobe.

"This was the first time that I ever designed a wardrobe for a computer-generated character. After the initial drawings were approved, the patterns were cut. Then the pieces were scanned onto the computer and sewn together in the software. I was asked to come back and help with the alterations, on screen! I'd look at the computer and tell them to raise the pants an inch or take in the waist a bit. So we were doing tailoring by computer. Clearly, this is a whole new venue for designers and, in some ways, it's a lot easier than working with live actors. Computer characters don't give you any grief."

—JOSEPH PORRO, COSTUME DESIGNER

Producer Douglas Wick, director Rob Minkoff, and costume designer Joseph Porro discuss wardrobe during preproduction.

MR. LITTLE
Fantastic . . . I hardly recognize you.

MRS. LITTLE
Very smart.

Mr. Little straightens Stuart's bow tie.

MR. LITTLE
And you look just like a Little.

STUART
I do? Good. I was worried I was going to look just like Ben.

CUT TO:

INT. FOYER – LITTLE HOUSE – SEVERAL DAYS LATER – EVENING

The extended Little clan has arrived in all its glory. BEATRICE, UNCLE STRETCH, EDGAR, SPENCER, ESTELLE, CRENSHAW, CRENSHAW'S WIFE crowd the foyer, all bearing GIFTS. All the male Littles wear bow ties. Mrs. Little greets everyone at the door.

MRS. CRENSHAW
The Littles are here!

MRS. LITTLE
Oh my goodness!

MR. LITTLE
Crenshaw!

CRENSHAW
Frederick!

MR. LITTLE
Little hi, Little lo!

ALL THE LITTLES
Little hey, Little ho!

BEATRICE carries an armload of wrapped presents.

"Stuart Little's clothes were the most expensive wardrobe in filmmaking history."

—JASON CLARK, EXECUTIVE PRODUCER

BEATRICE
We come bearing gifts for young Stuart.

EDGAR
Yes, where is my new nephew?

CRENSHAW
The Little family's getting bigger and bigger!

INT. LITTLE HOME – TOP OF THE STAIRS – CONTINUING
Stuart looks through the banister as all the greetings take place below.

STUART (*a little nervously*)
Boy, that's a lotta Littles.

MRS. CRENSHAW
Spencer, of course, almost got us lost.

UNCLE SPENCER
What do you mean, lost? No Little in the history of Littles has ever been lost on the way to this house! Remind me, where's the bathroom?

Everyone laughs. George enters from the basement.

GEORGE
Uncle Crenshaw!

UNCLE CRENSHAW (*picks up George*)
There's my favorite little nephew.

The extended Little family includes Brian Doyle-Murray, Jeffrey Jones, Connie Ray, Allyce Beasley, Estelle Getty, Harold Gould, and Patrick O'Brien.

UNCLE STRETCH
Oh, you can't say that anymore, Crenshaw.

MRS. CRENSHAW
That's right. Now we have two favorite little nephews.

EDGAR
That's right. Where is the lad?

UNCLE STRETCH
Yes. He's got a lot of gifts to open.

GEORGE (*re: gifts*)
Are any of those for me?

George leaves.

INT. FOYER – LITTLE HOUSE – CONTINUING
Stuart, now at the bottom of the stairs, tugs on Mr. Little's pant leg. Mr. Little looks down.

MR. LITTLE
Attention, everybody. We'd like to introduce you to someone.

MRS. LITTLE
This . . . is Stuart.

STUART
Hello, everyone.

THE VISUAL EFFECTS TEAM ON THE LIVE-ACTION SET

Work for the visual effects team began long before Stuart was in the film. In fact, the team was an essential part of the live-action shoot. Here they oversee the shot of the family party where Stuart is given human-size toys and voices his gratitude to all the Littles. In the final shot, as it appears on the film, Stuart walks through the scene in perfect harmony with his surroundings.

Dave Stump, Rob Minkoff (background), Roberto "Tito" Blasini, and Conor O'Gorman working on the set. For every visual effect, data was collected so that technicians could duplicate the shot for the digital production. The effects team needed to know details such as the kind of lens, camera angle, light source, and other such information so that when they created Stuart they could place him in a compatible environment.

Jerome Chen, Visual Effects Supervisor, makes sure that the camera angles will work when Stuart is added to the film at a later date. In the background is Uncle Stretch, played by the veteran actor Patrick O'Brien.

They all look in Stuart's direction. Then all, at the same time, lower their gaze to find him.

They stare slack-jawed at Stuart.

> EDGAR
> He's a—

> BEATRICE
> —dorable!

> MRS. CRENSHAW
> Adorable, yes.

Everyone agrees. Mr. and Mrs. Little are proud.

> EDGAR *(in the hubbub)*
> Adorable, that's right, I just couldn't think of the word.

CUT TO:

INT. LIVING ROOM – NIGHT
The Little family is gathered in the living room. Mrs. Little opens another present for Stuart.

> MRS.LITTLE
> Oh, Stuart! Look!

> MR. LITTLE
> Oh, Wow! Look at that? This is a real Schmelling.

> CRENSHAW
> It's a really new freak model.

> EDGAR
> I have one just like it at home.

> MRS. CRENSHAW
> We can all go bowling.

> MRS. LITTLE
> What a wonderful idea.

> UNCLE SPENCER
> I'll have to find my shoes.

Everyone admires the bowling ball. Mr. Little takes the ball, passes it to Crenshaw who then gives it to Mrs. Crenshaw.

> STRETCH
> Lookee here, Stuart. Climb on up here, son.

STRETCH rises, crosses to a normal-size boy's bicycle. Stuart looks up from his skis.

> STRETCH *(cont'd) (pats the bicycle seat)*
> Plant your caboose right up here.

TRUE STATISTICS

*D*uring production, the cast and crew consumed:

- —9,280 bagels
- —2,800 muffins
- —14,720 donuts
- —1,487 gallons of coffee
- —1,200 pounds of ribs

Stuart is sitting on the bicycle seat, which, of course, is way too big for him.

> AUNT BEATRICE
> Um . . . he may have to grow into it.

> MRS. CRENSHAW
> I think he's grown a little just since we've been here.

> LITTLES
> That's true, very true.

> STUART
> May I say something? In the orphanage, we used to tell fairy tales of finding our families and having a party like this. A party with cakes and presents and all varieties of meat loaf. A party with a big family who came from far away just to wish us well. I don't know much about families, but this must be the nicest family in the world, I think. So I just wanted to thank each of you. Because . . . now I know: Fairy tales are real.

The family cheers.

EXT. WINDOW SILL – LITTLE HOME – NIGHT
Snowbell's stomach is turning as he watches through the window.

> SNOWBELL
> Fairy tales are real? Oy! I think I'm gonna cough up a fur ball.

INT. LIVING ROOM – CONTINUOUS

WHY STUART ISN'T PERFECT

We tried very hard to avoid a "computery" feel to the way Stuart looks and moves. Sometimes there's a mathematical evenness to computer graphics that makes a character feel synthetic. It's like electronically generated music, which can be so unnervingly precise that our ear distinguishes it from something played live. We pick up these very subtle changes in measured time. It's the same thing with an animated character. There's a quality to the movement that we are trying to achieve that's not perfect . . . like life. There's a little bit of space between things and the intervals are not regular. None of us moves with the precision of a metronome and neither does Stuart.

—HENRY ANDERSON III, ANIMATION SUPERVISOR

CRENSHAW
And now, it's time for the best present of all. Something for you and George.

MR. LITTLE
George. Come on, stand next to Stuart.

He beckons to George to come join Stuart. George trudges toward them.

CRENSHAW
This is something that gave your father and me hours of enjoyment when we were young brothers just like you and Stuart.

Uncle Crenshaw takes out a baseball from his jacket pocket. Everyone "oohs."

CRENSHAW (cont'd)
This ball— belonged to your great, great-grandfather, Jedediah Little.

MR. LITTLE
He played a half-season for the Toledo Mud-Hens in 1901. He went oh-for fifty-eight. But he won a game by getting beaned with the bases loaded.

CRENSHAW
And this is the ball that beaned him.

Uncle Crenshaw gives the ball to George. George stares at the ball, Stuart looks at the ball.

EDGAR
George, why don't you take your brother outside and toss around the old horsehide.

CRENSHAW
Yeah, whaddya say George? You ready?

Pause.

GEORGE
Are you all nuts?

Gasp.

GEORGE (cont'd)
Bicycles, skis . . . Mice don't ski . . . How's he going to catch a watermelon? How's he gonna win a three-legged race? He's *not* my brother! He's a mouse!

LONG PAUSE

UNCLE STRETCH
Uh, time to go.

AUNT BEATRICE
Yes. Excellent idea!

UNCLE SPENCER
Good idea.

INT. LITTLES' BEDROOM – LATER
They're ASLEEP. Mrs. Little rolls over. There's a SQUEAL and then she SCREAMS, startled. Mr. Little then wakes with a shout.

The LIGHT GOES ON.

MRS. LITTLE
Stuart! Did I hurt you? What's the matter?

STUART
I . . . I just wanted to ask you something, but you were already asleep . . .

MR. LITTLE
What did you want to ask us?

STUART
About . . . my real family. You know, the ones I look like.

A long silence. Mrs. Little is too hurt to speak.

> MRS. LITTLE
> He hates us!

> MR. LITTLE
> We've never been hated before.

> STUART
> No, no, no! It's not that. It's not that at all.

Beat. Mrs. Little gets a grip on herself.

> STUART *(cont'd)*
> It's just that . . . something's missing. I feel an empty space inside me . . . And I just want to know what was there before.

> MRS. LITTLE
> You have an empty space? That's so sad!

Mrs. Little's eyes fill with water.

> STUART
> Oh dear. *(she fights tears)* I hope I haven't left you dismayed and disappointed.

> MR. LITTLE
> No, no, no, no . . . we don't feel dismayed and disappointed.

> MRS. LITTLE
> Not at all.

> STUART
> Are you sure?

> MR. LITTLE
> We're certain, Stuart. And if you want us to, we'll find out about your real parents.

> MRS. LITTLE *(holding back tears)*
> Mm hmm.

> STUART
> Well . . . Good night then.

CUT TO:

INT. ADOPTION OFFICE – DAY

Mrs. Keeper stares across her desk.

> MRS. KEEPER
> It's out of the question and it's against the rules. *(beat)*
> Besides, it's very hard to track mouse families . . . They're not good with paper work.

> MRS. LITTLE
> But he has an empty space.

Mr. and Mrs. Little pause, conflicted. Keeper leans in.

> MRS. KEEPER
> Are there problems with Stuart?

> MR. LITTLE
> No . . . not at all.

MRS. KEEPER'S OFFICE

The set for Mrs. Keeper's office was also meant to show a world without color where children are warehoused. Even though she probably has a lot of love for the kids, she is overwhelmed by how many children are in her care. The file-cabinet wall, for example, was visually over the top. She's the keeper of thousands and thousands of files on kids and mice and probably other animals, too.

—BILL BRZESKI, PRODUCTION DESIGNER

MRS. LITTLE
No . . . there've been a few . . .

MR. LITTLE
Difficulties.

MRS. LITTLE
Difficulties.

MRS. KEEPER
Difficulties . . .

MRS. LITTLE
Little things . . .

Mrs. Little squirms, too honest to leave this out:

MR. LITTLE
I mean . . . there . . .

MRS. LITTLE
Well, the cat tried to eat him when we first brought him home.

MR. LITTLE
He spat the boy right out in a heckava jiffy.

Keeper nods, unimpressed. Mrs. Little can't stop herself:

MRS. LITTLE *(cont'd)*
And . . . um . . . he did spend a brief time trapped in the family washing machine.

MR. LITTLE
It turns out he's quite a fine swimmer!

The Littles sag. They know how bad this looks.

MR. LITTLE *(cont'd) (humbly)*
Mrs. Keeper, he wants to know about his family. Any child would have questions about that.

MRS. KEEPER
Yes . . .

MR. LITTLE
So you'll look into this for us, won't you.

MRS. KEEPER
I'll certainly try.

MR. LITTLE
Well, it would mean a lot to him.

Mr. and Mrs. Little get up to leave.

MRS. LITTLE
Thank you, Mrs. Keeper.

MR. LITTLE
Thank you.

MRS. KEEPER
Not at all . . . As soon as I have something, I'll let you know.

She studies them; their discomfort is obvious.

CUT TO:
INT. PANTRY – LITTLE HOME – DAY
Snowbell eats out of his dish. STUART ENTERS. Then:

"Most of Stuart's problems derive from his size. He gets into a lot of vertically challenged situations. . . . As far as height is concerned, Stuart and I are really at opposite ends of the spectrum, so I can relate to his problems."

—GEENA DAVIS

STUART
Hey, Snow . . . I know that you and I got off on the wrong paw . . . and I just wanted to see if we could start off fresh . . . You know, clean slate . . . what do you say . . . want to be friends?

SNOWBELL
Um . . . No.

STUART
Okay then . . .

Snowbell walks away.

INT. KITCHEN – DAY
Snowbell pads from the pantry into the kitchen, scowling.

SNOWBELL
Friends? Pardon me while I puke. I'd be the laughingstock of the Upper West Side.

Suddenly, there's a tapping on the window. Startled, Snowbell looks up, sees Monty, a scrawny alley cat, outside the window, scratching to get in. Snowbell gulps.

MONTY
Hey, Snow . . . Let me in. I'm starvin'! What's in the dish today? Wet food? Dry food? Little kibble?

SNOWBELL
Oh, no! Monty the Mouth!!

MONTY
Come on, Snowy buddy. Come on, let me in!

Executive producer Jason Clark and director Rob Minkoff on the set during the shooting of the Central Park scenes.

HANDLING STUART LITTLE, THE ACTOR

Overall, Stuart has been handling the stardom thing quite well. Granted, it's a little difficult for young actors like him who make this meteoric rise to stardom and find there are real issues they still have to work out. Sometimes it's hard to get him on the set, but once he's there, he really gives his all. There have been a couple of late mornings when we had to track him down. You know, he is part of the new rat pack and it's been hard to pull him out of that. We had to bring him back from Vegas once. Otherwise, though, he's been okay.

—JASON CLARK, EXECUTIVE PRODUCER

SNOWBELL *(to Monty)*
Go away. There's no food here.

MONTY
Please . . .

SNOWBELL
Shoo!

Snowbell sees Monty's back end disappear from the window.

Monty suddenly leaps through the cat door, right into the kitchen.

MONTY
You know, I'm not picky . . . As long as it ain't meat loaf. That stuff gives me gas somethin' awful.

SNOWBELL
Sorry, it's meat loaf.

MONTY
Oh, well. Beggars can't be choosers. Load me up and light a match . . .

Monty beelines for the pantry.

Snowbell follows Monty to the pantry door.

SNOWBELL
Oh, no, no, Monty! Stop! Wait! Don't go in there! That room's a mess! It's . . . hey—

MONTY
Outta my way!

SNOWBELL
Have you heard the one about the cat, the dog, and the buffalo? And they all walk into a bar, ha ha . . .

Monty scoots inside the pantry.

SNOWBELL (cont'd)
Oh great, what am I going to tell him now?

Snowbell rushes after him in a panic.

SNOWBELL (cont'd)
Monty, I can explain . . . I . . . He's a . . .

INT. PANTRY
Snowbell rushes into the pantry and sees Monty chowing down at his bowl . . . but no *Stuart!* What a break.

MONTY
Explain what?

SNOWBELL
Explain that . . . explain that you should stuff your face.

MONTY
Oh, thanks.

Snowbell joins Monty on the other side of the dish.

SNOWBELL
Monty, I don't want to rush you, but you really have to leave. The Littles are due back any minute and you know what happened last time.

MONTY (eating)
Hey, nature called — I answered. Besides, a little club soda will take that stain right out.

Snowbell looks past Monty's shoulder and sees a box of Ritz crackers being walked across the countertop . . . Stuart! Snowbell's eyes bulge at the sight. Monty catches a glimpse of Snowbell's startled expression.

MONTY (smacking his lips)
Hey Snow, what's wrong with your eyes?

SNOWBELL
My eyes? Nothing.

MONTY
You know, you're acting kind of strange. What is it? Worms? Fleas? Yeah, you look pale. Maybe you should see a vet.

SNOWBELL
A vet. What a swell idea. Do you know anybody?

Monty turns, but the box is gone. All he sees is the kitchen door swing.

MONTY
What was that?

SNOWBELL
What was that what?

MONTY
What was that? What?

INT. KITCHEN
Snowbell and Monty emerge into the kitchen and stop at the kitty door.

Todd Wilderman sketch of Snowbell trying to hide Stuart from his pals.

MONTY
Well, I hate to eat and run.

SNOWBELL
No, no please, by all means . . . run.

Monty leaves through the kitty door, then unexpectedly pops his head back in.

SNOWBELL (cont'd)
Phew, that was close.

MONTY
Hey, Snow, I almost forgot to thank you.

STUART'S TRAILER

One of the perks for a leading actor in a feature film is a comfortable trailer where the star can relax, read, and have some privacy from other cast members and the crew. The production company for *Stuart Little* saved a great deal of money because their leading man required only a modified trailer. "Most of the talent on the film had very big trailers but not Stuart," explains producer Douglas Wick. "We only had to provide him with this really tiny trailer; we saved the production a lot of money and that was very positive."

Monty looks up and spots Stuart's tail wiggling into the box of crackers which sit on the counter.

MONTY (cont'd)
Hey —

SNOWBELL
Ahhgh.

MONTY
What the . . . !

SNOWBELL
Oh, no.

MONTY'S POV
Monty leaps up and knocks the box over, spilling its contents, including Stuart.

Seeing Monty, Stuart looks up and smiles brightly.

STUART
Oh, hello! You must be a friend of Snowbell's. I'm Stuart.

MONTY
Aren't you gonna run?

Stuart's costar Jonathan Lipnicki waits while Stuart changes clothes in his trailer.

STUART
Why?

MONTY
'Cause you're a mouse.

STUART
I'm not just a mouse, I'm also a member of this family.

MONTY
A mouse with a pet cat?

Monty starts to chuckle. Then laughs harder. More laughter. Stuart ponders it for a moment. Then:

STUART
I, I guess that is pretty funny.

Monty is in hysterics.

MONTY
Pretty funny?! I'm gonna wet my fur! A mouse with a pet cat! *(to Snowbell, laughing)* Your new little master! Wait till the boys hear about this!

Finally, Snowbell can't take it anymore.

SNOWBELL *(to Stuart)*
Oh, the humiliation. I'M GOING TO KILL YOU!

He erupts, leaping at Stuart, claws extended.

STUART
Oh, dear.

Snowbell hops up onto the countertop and chases Stuart out of the pantry. Stuart runs for his life.

SNOWBELL
Come back here!

INT. KITCHEN – DAY
Stuart sees a SHIRT HANGING from an ironing board. He climbs up the shirt on to the board.

Snowbell gets trapped under the shirt, struggles to free himself.

SNOWBELL
What the . . .

Snowbell leaps on to the board, tipping it and catapulting Stuart against the wall, then on to the top of a flip-top GARBAGE CAN.

Snowbell leaps at him.

SNOWBELL
Aarrgghh!

Stuart jumps, landing on the garbage can pedal, which causes the lid to go up.

Snowbell's anger turns to terror.

SNOWBELL (cont'd)
Aaaaahhhhhh!!!

Snowbell flies into the trashcan, the lid slams down on top of him.

Beat. Snowbell's head pushes the lid up.

SNOWBELL
All right. No more Mr. Nice Kitty.

Snowbell resumes the chase. Stuart eludes him by squeezing under a door just in time.

SNOWBELL (cont'd)
Hey, come back here. You can't go in there. That's George's room. Hey, come on. Come on out here. You forgot something. You forgot to get killed.

INT. BASEMENT – MOMENTS LATER
Stuart emerges from under the door, steps on a rollerskate and tumbles down the cellar steps.

STUART'S POV – THE BASEMENT
This is the workshop of an artist . . . In every corner, we see MINIATURES, each built by hand: Tiny cars, horses and wagons, city streets with shops and people, a hydroelectric dam, an electric train . . . He lands in the middle of a Western town. He is dazzled.

GEORGE
What are you doing here?

STUART
I just thought I'd drop in. Did you build all these?

GEORGE
Me and my Dad.

STUART
Wow, it's incredible. It's like being in a real live western. Howdy, Partner. Draw, you lily-livered, yellow-bellied son of a one-eyed prairie dog . . . (ad-lib gun noises)

GEORGE
I'm trying to concentrate!

STUART
Oh. Sorry . . . (excited) Is that a train?

GEORGE
What does it look like, Picklehead?

STUART
Can we play with it? Please, please, please, please, please.

CUT TO:
STUART APPARENTLY TIED TO THE TRACKS. THE TRAIN IS MOVING.

STUART
Help! Somebody! Help me!

The train is getting close to Stuart.

STUART (cont'd)
Help! Please! Somebody! Help me! Please!

Then we see that Stuart actually isn't tied down. He has wrapped his tail around himself to make it look as if he's tied. He jumps off the tracks just in time as George yells with excitement. The train passes.

STUART (proudly)
Ta-da! Thank you, thank you very much, thank you, thank you.

George laughs and applauds.

GEORGE
You're crazy!

George stops the train.

GEORGE (cont'd)
Hey. I have an idea.

George displays a miniature classic car.

GEORGE (cont'd)
Hop in.

STUART
Wow, great car, George.

GEORGE
Yeah. It's my favorite.

So Stuart steps into the tiny car, sits comfortably . . . and immediately LOOKS LIKE HE MIGHT CRY.

GEORGE
Stuart, what's wrong?

STUART
Nothing, I . . . *(how to put this?)* It's just . . . It's the first time I've fit in since I got here. What's that?

Stuart gets out of the Roadster, and walks toward an UNFINISHED MODEL BOAT. George tightens a bit.

Her name is the *Wasp,* and she's the start of something magnificent. Stuart stares, dazzled by the craftsmanship. Even unfinished like this, she's a gem.

GEORGE
Oh. That . . . That's the *Wasp.*

STUART *(breathless)*
She's beautiful.

GEORGE
Yeah, but she's not finished.

STUART
When are you going to finish it?

GEORGE
Well, me and my dad were building her but . . . I decided to stop.

STUART
How come?

GEORGE
I'm too little for a race like that.

STUART
Little? You're not little. Not to me.

GEORGE
Stuart, you've never seen one of these races. There're hundreds of people there. Everybody from school. I mean . . . *(has to say it)* What if she lost?

Silence. George shrinks a bit, way too exposed. Stuart crosses to the *Wasp*'s starboard gunwale, studying him.

STUART *(gently)*
At least she'll have *been* somewhere. Come on, George. What do you say? Let's get started.

Pause while George looks at Stuart and thinks.

GEORGE
You know I'm not really sure I want a brother.

STUART
Oh . . . Well, how about a friend?

Pause.

GEORGE
I guess I can always use a friend.

Close-up of the basement set where Stuart discovers George's trains and the Wasp. *In the foreground is a western town, behind which is the Alpine set. In the background are stairs leading into the basement. All of these sets were built as elaborate miniature sets and installed by Imageworks' physical-production department.*

Stuart SMILES.

INT. LIVING ROOM – DAY
Snowbell saunters in as Mrs. Little and Mr. Little arrive home from seeing Mrs. Keeper. They're both a little glum.

> **MR. & MRS. LITTLE** *(looking for him)*
> Stuart? Stuart? Stuart? Stuart?

Mrs. Little opens the basement door.

> **MR. LITTLE**
> George?

> **GEORGE** (O.S.) *(from basement)*
> Yes, Dad.

"As a child, you're looking at the world at knee level and it seems scary and over-whelming. Watching the heroics of someone three inches tall can be very inspiring."
—DOUGLAS WICK, PRODUCER

> **MRS. LITTLE**
> Have you seen Stuart?

> **GEORGE** (O.S.)
> He's down here. With me.

Mrs. Little and Mr. Little look at each other, alarmed.

> **MR. LITTLE**
> What are you doing to him?

They open the door to the basement and hurry down.

INT. BASEMENT – DAY
Mr. Little and Mrs. Little race down the stairs, then stop in surprise. They can't quite believe what they're seeing—George and Stuart, working together, huddled over the *Wasp*.

> **GEORGE**
> He's helping me finish the *Wasp*.

Mr. Little and Mrs. Little's jaws drop.

> **MR. LITTLE** *(stammering)*
> That's, that's wonderful, Son. That's terrific.

> **STUART**
> Can't race her like this, right, George?

GEORGE
Right.

Mr. Little and Mrs. Little can barely reply. They're too thrilled.

MRS. LITTLE
When's the next race?

GEORGE *(petrified)*
Two days.

MR. LITTLE
Two days?

STUART
We'll be ready.

EXT. LITTLE HOUSE – DAY
Snowbell stares in through the basement window, watching Stuart and George working together as friends. He lets out a soft wail of jealousy.

INT. BASEMENT

MR. LITTLE
Well, how about we all go together.

MRS. LITTLE
That's a wonderful idea . . . if it's all right with the boys.

STUART *(cont'd) (proudly)*
It'll be our first family outing.

We PULL BACK as Stuart and George dive into work,

their parents happily leaving them to it . . .

DISSOLVE TO:

EXT. LITTLE HOUSE – DAY
Snowbell stares in through the basement window, watching Stuart and George working together as friends. He lets out a soft wail of jealousy.

EXT. ALLEY – NIGHT
Snowbell and Monty stand there amid the PUDDLES and TRASH.

MONTY
I'm telling ya, Snowy. This guy can fix anything.

SNOWBELL
I don't know, Monty. Maybe this isn't such a good idea.

MONTY
Quit being such a scaredy-cat. Now you want to get rid of the mouse or not?

SNOWBELL
Of course I do.

MONTY
All right, then. Hey, hey, Smokey. Smokey, hey, it's me. It's me, Monty.

Smokey, a tough-looking cat steps out of the shadows.

Drawing by Michael Scheffe illustrating an early concept (that was not used) where Stuart flies one of George's planes.

SMOKEY
What is it now?

MONTY
Well, my friend, Snowbell here, needs a favor.

Smokey looks Snowbell up and down.

SMOKEY
Snowbell, now there's a manly name.

Monty LAUGHS.

MONTY *(laughing)*
Smokey's funny.

SNOWBELL *(nervous laugh)*
Yeah. You see, sir. I've got this mouse at home
I can't eat.

SMOKEY
Sensitive stomach?

SNOWBELL
No. I can't eat him 'cause he's a member of the
family.

SMOKEY
A mouse with a pet cat?

Monty laughs.

MONTY *(amused)*
Isn't that funny?

SMOKEY
That's not funny. That's sick. A cat can't have a
rodent for a master. I mean, what's this world
coming to? It's against the laws of nature. Word
of this gets out, it'll be bad for cats all over.

SNOWBELL
So you think you can help me?

SMOKEY
Consider it done.

SNOWBELL
Thank you, sir. Thank you, Mr. Smokey, sir. You've
saved my life.

Smokey climbs to the top of the boxes.

SMOKEY
Don't worry, Tinkerbell. I'm all over it.

Snowbell chuckles.

SNOWBELL *(laughing)*
Tinkerbell! He called me Tinkerbell. That's funny!

SMOKEY
Yeah, right, whatever.

SNOWBELL
You're a funny guy. We gotta hang out more often.

Smokey leaves.

EXT. CENTRAL PARK – POND – DAY
A CROWD is gathering. Six model boats float in the Central Park POND. They're all store-bought, all impressive, and each of them has caretakers and a captain.

CUT TO:

EXT. STARTER'S LINE – MORNING
The *Wasp* is mounted on two pieces of wood by the edge of the water. *Stuart is aboard,* thrilled to be helping. George fiddles with the boat's remote control.

GEORGE
Anchor up.

STUART
Check.

GEORGE
Stays all battened.

STUART
Check.

GEORGE
Rudder.

George hits a button on the control. The rudder responds.

STUART
Check.

GEORGE
Sail.

The sail folds and unfolds.

STUART
Check.

GEORGE
Firn line.

STUART
Check.

ANGLE ON MR. AND MRS. LITTLE

MRS. LITTLE
They're doing checks.

MR. LITTLE
George, Stuart, would you like a hot dog?

GEORGE & STUART
Check.

Mr. and Mrs. Little head toward the concession stand.

RACE STARTER *(to other race official)*
All set to get underway.
(into microphone, O.S.)
Welcome everyone to the annual Central Park boat race. We will be casting off in five minutes.

ANGLE ON STUART. He stands in the hatch of the *Wasp.*

STUART
Well, everything appears to be in shipshape, but to be on the safe side, I better check the hull for leaks.

He closes the hatch. George looks up.

A boat passes, REVEALING the *Womrath,* which is by far the largest and most impressive craft out here.

GEORGE
Oh no, Anton.

ANTON
Gee, George, what did you do, get that out of a cereal box?

Anton walks over to George.

ANTON *(cont'd)*
I'm glad you're here, George. *Someone's* gotta finish last.

Anton leaves as Mr. and Mrs. Little come back. Mr. Little recognizes Anton from the toy store.

MR. LITTLE
I don't like that child.

MRS. LITTLE
Hmm.

Stuart pops his head out from below deck.

Mr. Little offers George a hot dog. He just stares.

MR. LITTLE
George, not hungry?

GEORGE
No.

Mrs. Little offers a hot dog to Stuart.

MRS. LITTLE
Stuart?

STUART
I'm not hungry either.

CUT TO:
George and Mr. Little carry the *Wasp* to the water.

GEORGE *(to Stuart)*
Stuart, could you get the remote?

Thor Freudenthal storyboard of Snowbell and Monty walking the streets of Manhattan. In the final film, this scene looks remarkably similar to Thor's drawing.

Snowbell had several friends in the neighborhood. Some of them were house cats, others were store cats. He knew a Maltese cat in the A&P, a white Persian in the apartment house next door, a tortoise-shell in the delicatessen, a tiger cat in the basement of the branch library, and a beautiful young Angora who had escaped from a cage in a pet shop on Third Avenue and had gone to live a free life of her own in the tool house of the small park near Stuart's home.

—E. B. WHITE, *STUART LITTLE*, 1945

STUART
Aye aye, Captain!

George and Mr. Little lower the *Wasp* into the water.

MR. LITTLE
Wow. Doesn't she look great? You okay?

GEORGE
Maybe we should go home.

MR. LITTLE
Why?

GEORGE
I'm not wearing my lucky underwear.

MR. LITTLE
You don't have lucky underwear.

GEORGE
Well, maybe we should get some and come back for another race.

Stuart struggles with the remote.

MR. LITTLE
George, listen, I know how worried you are about losing, believe me. But you know what we say, the thing that really matters is to never stop trying, okay.

GEORGE
Okay.

MR. LITTLE
That's the spirit.

Stuart struggles with the remote. He staggers slightly under the weight of it. No one notices as Stuart stumbles into a walking lane along the pond. Pedestrians buzz by him. He dodges one, then another, *his vision entirely blocked by the remote.*

RACE STARTER
Everyone to your places. The race is about to start.

Then one particularly HARRIED PEDESTRIAN hurries by, and Stuart is sent flying.

The remote flies out of his hands . . . A MAN WEARING HUGE BOOTS DOESN'T SEE IT ON THE GROUND.

MRS. LITTLE
Where's Stuart?!

STUART
Look out, Sir!!!

Mrs. Little appears behind George and Mr. Little.

George and the Littles turn when they hear the CRUNCH. Four faces sink at once — George worst of all. Stuart turns, speechless.

MRS. LITTLE
Stuart, are you hurt?

MR. LITTLE
Stuart, what happened?

STUART
It was completely my fault. I couldn't grip it.

George picks up the broken remote.

Then, a sharp, cackling sound — ANTON'S LAUGHTER — is heard from across the Pond. He points and laughs.

George wants to die. Stuart too. The Littles sag.

George turns and runs away, devastated. Mrs. and Mrs. Little share a concerned look. Mrs. Little goes after George.

George is sitting on a nearby bench.

Mrs. Little kneels in front of George, trying:

MRS. LITTLE
Oh honey, everything will be all right.

GEORGE
No it won't.

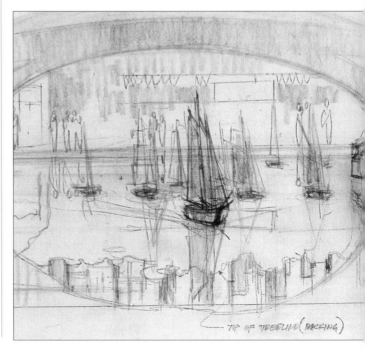

THE CENTRAL PARK STAGE

For the production design, the biggest challenge in the movie was creating the Central Park set. Trying to re-create a real outdoor setting on a stage is the hardest thing for a production designer to do. The lighting alone is very difficult. We decided, throughout the movie, that the basic look of the film would have an old-fashioned movie quality, in the style of *The Wizard of Oz* or Vincent Minnelli musicals. We didn't pretend to be any place other than a big stage, making a big-scale movie. Everything is on the oversize scale of a lavish Hollywood movie.

—BILL BRZESKI, PRODUCTION DESIGNER

Below: Stuart's boat race scene begins and ends on the bridge above the pond. In its earliest stages, the bridge was drawn in pencil (left). The final structure came out looking almost exactly like those early drawings. Right: The background for the bridge from this view (above) was a blue screen. Later (below), the skyline of Manhattan was added to the film.

MRS. LITTLE
Maybe we can fix it, huh? A little glue, who'll know?

GEORGE
Mom.

Stuart sits dejected next to Mr. Little at the pond's edge.

STUART
This is awful. Our first family outing. I've ruined everything.

MR. LITTLE
Well, you know Stuart, these things happen.

STUART
But, what about George . . .

MR. LITTLE
George'll be fine . . .

Mr. Little looks over and sees Mrs. Little's beckoning glance.

MR. LITTLE (cont'd)
I'll be right back.

Mr. Little walks away from Stuart and approaches his wife and George.

Stuart eyes George, feeling awful. Then he eyes the *Wasp.*

Mr. Little bends down to George.

MR. LITTLE (cont'd)
George, you know what? I really think . . .

RACE STARTER (O.S)
All boats to their marks! Ready! And . . . Go!

The Race Starter's horn blares.

We hear SQUEALS OF EXCITEMENT as the race begins . . . cheering, yelling.

ASSORTED KIDS & PARENTS (O.S.)
Look at her go, Mom! Hey, watch where you're going! Mine's the fastest, mine's the fastest!

Mr. Little loses his confidence.

RACE STARTER
And the race is on. Looks as though everyone got off to a clean start. It's a beautiful blustery day for sailing . . .

MR. LITTLE
I think we should just go home.

RACE STARTER
Sails are full and there's a mouse on that boat?!

And:

George and his parents freeze.

LITTLES
Stuart!

EXT. ON THE POND – CONTINUING
George leads the way as the Littles push through the crowd of spectators and skippers at the edge of the pond. There sails the *Wasp* with Stuart at the helm.

GEORGE
STUART!

STUART
GEORGE!

GEORGE
What are you doing?

Stuart looks up in response to George's call.

STUART
Sailing . . . I hope.

Mr. and Mrs. Little fight their way along the bank of the pond.

MRS. LITTLE
Stuart, you come back here this minute.

STUART
I can't.

MRS. LITTLE
Why not?

STUART
I don't know how.

EXT. SIDE OF POND
The *Wasp*'s sail swings over Stuart's head, sending the boat in the opposite direction.

Stuart gains control and turns the *Wasp* into the path of the competitors heading toward the bridge.

MRS. LITTLE
Frederick, I don't like this one bit.

MR. LITTLE
Stuart, your mother doesn't like this one bit.

STUART
I'm okay, Mom.

Above: Rob Minkoff directs Jonathan Lipnicki on the Central Park set. Below: Jonathan Lipnicki talking to his invisible costar, Stuart Little, who will eventually appear on the deck of the Wasp.

MARTY KLINE ON MATTE PAINTING

To expand the stylized world of *Stuart Little,* we used several kinds of digital matte paintings. Throughout film history, from early glass shots and hanging miniatures to today's 3-D digital matte paintings, artists have been called upon to enlarge the scope of original photography, particularly to alter reality to support the creative vision of the director. Matte paintings are always trying to strike a balance between authenticity (the design that is the world in which our story takes place) and reality (the elements that make an image believable to the audience as a real place). The freedom, flexibility, and creativity of today's digital tools have greatly enhanced the artist's ability to create environments unique and specific to the story. Matte paintings help alter the audience's perception of the world in which our characters live.

The world of *Stuart Little* is a stylized reality, established as a story set in New York City but infused with a stylized appearance. Working closely with the production design team, our art department at Imageworks produced a lot of concept sketches to help the director define the New York look more precisely. As a basis, we referred to many images from the '30s, '40s, and '50s. The production designer, Bill Brzeski, encouraged us to apply this period look to create a New York of contemporary scale but period style. Ultimately, we determined that a "too stylized" New York might not be easily recognizable to the audience as New York, and we adopted a more normal contemporary look. This was especially true of the skyline shots, where we kept many buildings that are recognized around the world as New York.

We used about twenty matte paintings in the movie. Some were composed from still photography, some from film plates, some were digital originals, and many were a combination of images. The establishing shot for the Central Park Boat Pond, for example, began as a series of roughs from various angles that showed the basic elements—the city, the park, and the boat pond—as modified for our story. The stage design had used the conservatory pond as a starting point, adding a bridge that Stuart could sail under to allow the majority of the race to take place on the reservoir. With those great images we began the process of refining the matte shot for the specific requirements of our action. A very important issue for Rob was to maintain a centrally symmetrical feeling that had been established in the opening shot and at the Littles' house.

In order to create a symmetrical Central Park of *Stuart Little* proportions, we sent a photographer, Richard Lund, up in a helicopter over Central Park to shoot the appropriate still photos. We had already done a digital model to determine where to shoot, and how to assemble the pieces, but that was only a tiny portion of the work for Bob Scifo, the matte painter for this shot. Major changes were made to the proportions of the park. Subtle changes to the boat pond and its placement were required. To enhance the transition to stage scenes, the painting was projected onto 3-D geometry and given a sense of movement, a push-in, with perspective shifts that provided an increased feeling of depth and reality.

Given the perspective of a story told largely from the point of view of a three-inch leading character, the actual distance from one side of Central Park to the other was far too great. Through matte painting and scenic back-

Finished view of Central Park as it is featured in the movie. Many of the proportions were changed to fit the mouselike perspective required by the script.

ings, we were able to bring the park into perspective. Without the scenic touch of a matte painting the park would have been bewilderingly large.

In another example, also from the boat race sequence, we employed a painted scenic backing to surround the perimeter of the boat pond set built on Stage 30. But when the camera turns to the family on the bridge for the scene's major moment, we needed a matte painting, to keep us in our magical New York.

We had planned to paint the New York City backgrounds across the river from Stout World but ultimately used film plates shot by John Dykstra on location. It was agreed that no major redesign of the city was required here, only enhancements from recompositing film elements. These film elements were tiled together on a simulated 3-D dome in the computer. Then we moved the camera around the dome as the shot required to give us the illusion of continuity. By tiling film plates, the action in the background, such as cars driving on shoreline or water flowing in the river, seemed continuous. In this process, you want the background to have some life but not so much as to distract from the characters or the main action of the scene.

Matte painting is a very involved process that requires a lot of advance planning, but it can produce amazing results. The beauty of this process is that we can complete things that couldn't have been photographed with the set, adding a lot to the flexibility of the filmmaking process.

—MARTY KLINE, VISUAL EFFECTS ART DIRECTOR

ERIC ALLARD ON THE BOATS

Our biggest mechanical effects scenes were for the boat race. There were several scenes in which Stuart is manipulating various things on the boat—moving the steering wheel, the sails, and so on. We had to build these things and make them move by themselves.

I suggested early on to the director that the boats for our regatta should be akin to the cars in *The Great Race,* a variety of different shapes, sizes, and colors. He liked the idea, so that is how we created our fleet of boats. Our remote-control boats had sails that looked like they were inflated by the wind when, really, there was no wind. We created a track system that was secured to the pond subfloor. Cable-winch-driven travelers were attached to the boats in such a way that the boats looked like they were sailing. However, when the director yelled "Cut!," we could reverse the switches and the boats rolled back to their starting positions. Then we did the whole thing again, probably about a hundred times during the course of filming. When we got into the main action of the race, after the boats leave the park setting, we shot second-unit visual effects in a tank that was built on the Paramount Studios back lot. The boat race involved lots of collisions and tangled rigging, most of which was accomplished on tracks with the track system.

Later Stuart was composited into the shot and the two elements interacted.

There's a lot of planning in making a movie like *Stuart Little.* We had storyboards for every frame of film that we were going to shoot. We spent months going over the boards and making sure that every department knew its responsibility for each shot.

GEORGE
Go, Stuart!

EXT. BRIDGE
The Littles ascend onto the bridge and watch as Stuart's boat passes below.

RACE STARTER
We've got some mighty fine sailing vessels spreading their stuff today. The biggest of them all is the *Womrath.*

GEORGE
Come on, Stuart!

George switches to other side right next to Anton.

ANTON
Gee, George . . . you all done crying?

GEORGE
Yeah. You all done being a jerk?

ANTON *(not realizing what he's saying)*
No . . .

EXT. BRIDGE
George and Mr. and Mrs. Little look out to see the *Wasp.*

MRS. LITTLE
Frederick, what if he falls?

MR. LITTLE
Remember . . . he's quite a fine swimmer.

Mrs. Little shoots him a look.

MR. LITTLE *(cont'd)*
Stuart, be careful, now.

STUART
I will, Dad!

EXT. POND

We tilt up to see the *Wasp* trailing the rest of the pack out into the BIG POND.

The Pack with the *Womrath* in the lead sails past. The *Wasp,* in the back of the pack, seems to be gaining.

EXT. POND

A competitor's boat is about to overtake the *Womrath.*

EXT. BRIDGE

Anton swings his control stick.

EXT. POND

The *Womrath* swings to block the passing boat and causes a collision.

EXT. BRIDGE

Kids react to the collision.

The skipper of the mangled boat turns to face Anton.

> **SKIPPER**
> Hey, that's cheating! You can't do that!

> **ANTON**
> Well, I just did.

Anton nods to one of his toadies and the toadie removes the skipper.

The Littles see the *Wasp* heading for the disabled boats.

EXT. POND

Stuart shoves the wheel hard to starboard. Stuart manages to avoid the tangle of boats and stay in the race.

He swings to the inside aiming directly at the buoy.

The *Wasp* and the *Womrath* go into the turn with *Womrath* on the outside, but in the lead. The *Wasp* is on the inside turning tightly and suddenly Stuart hikes out.

He was proud of his ability with boats and liked to show off.
—E. B. WHITE, *STUART LITTLE,* 1945

EXT. BRIDGE

> **MRS. LITTLE**
> What's he doing?

> **MR. LITTLE**
> I think he's hiking out.

> **MRS. LITTLE**
> Well, tell him to stop it.

> **MR. LITTLE**
> No, that's a good thing.

> **MRS. LITTLE**
> Oh. Good hiking out, Stuart.

EXT. POND

The *Wasp* begins to pull even with the *Womrath.*

EXT. BRIDGE

Anton wiggles the levers of his remote.

> **ANTON**
> I hope that mouse can swim.

Here are six of the ten boats that competed in the Central Park race. In all, a fleet of twenty boats was built for the race. Although there were only ten model boats in the race, for every boat a backup was built, just in case anything happened during filming. "And something always happens," notes Eric Allard. "In the long run, it's cheaper [from a production standpoint] to build a backup and have it on hand than to have to halt production during the shoot while another boat is made."

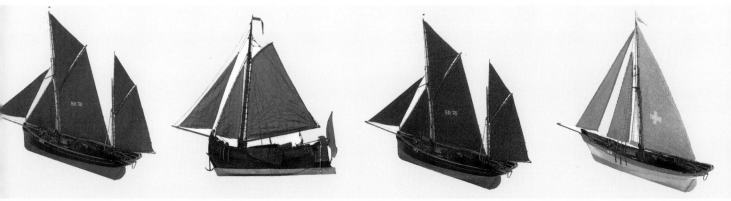

George tries to grab the remote, which Anton pulls away. A toadie steps in front of George, staring him down.

GEORGE (panic)
Stuart, look out!

George jumps on Anton.

EXT. POND
The *Womrath* swerves toward the *Wasp* as it is passing.

EXT. POND
The boats collide. The *Wasp* shudders as the mainmast tangles with the top rigging on the *Womrath*.

EXT. POND
The *Womrath*'s booms begin to swing back and forth. As the booms swing, the *Womrath*'s mainsail gets slightly torn.

EXT. BRIDGE

ADD BEAT OF ANTON STILL WORKING REMOTE WITH SOME DIALOGUE OF CONCERN, RE: TORN MAINSAIL

EXT. POND
STUART — Swings around high above the decks and jumps from the line to the top of the *Wasp*'s mast.

THE BOATS — Separate and the *Wasp* whips away and Stuart takes a wild ride on the top of the mast.

EXT. BRIDGE

ANTON (shouting)
Look what that stupid mouse did to my sail.

GEORGE
He's not a stupid mouse.

ANTON
You're right. He's a stupid rat!

EXT. POND
The *Womrath* and the *Wasp* are close, but the *Womrath* has a slight lead.

EXT. BRIDGE
Mr. and Mrs. Little step in to separate George and Anton.

MRS. LITTLE
Oh!

MR. LITTLE
Hey, hey, hey. Come on. Hey, what's going on here? George!

EXT. BRIDGE
Mrs. Little looks up to the boats.

MRS. LITTLE
STUART!

EXT. POND
Stuart at the wheel, sees the tangled rigging.

EXT. POND
Stuart finishes climbing the mast of the *Womrath* and begins to hand over hand along the rigging to where the *Wasp*'s mast is snagged.

EXT. POND
Anton's boat is stuck. Stuart untangles the rigging.

EXT. BRIDGE
Anton wildly works his remote control in an effort to free the *Womrath* from the *Wasp*.

EXT. POND
Suddenly the *Womrath*'s mainsail tear splits wide open and she veers off course directly into the path of the *Wasp*.

EXT. BRIDGE
Anton struggles with his remote in a futile attempt to regain control.

ANTON
What's happening?

"Away the boats are sailing toward the north end of the pond. It's a magnificent site, with seagulls whelling and crying overhead. . . . The boats are getting a strong assist from the wind off Seventy-second Street. The west wind, which has come halfway across the Central Park Basin — you know, you can almost hear it whistle through the rigging as it blows spray across the gleaming rocks."

—ADAPTED FROM THE BOOK, THIS DESCRIPTION OF THE RACE WAS READ BY STAN FREBERG, WHO DID THE VOICE-OVER FOR THE RACE ANNOUNCER

EXT. POND

Stuart sees the impending crash and jumps from the mast onto the sail and slides down landing on the deck next to the wheel. He spins the wheel of the *Wasp* and narrowly misses the careening *Womrath*.

EXT. BRIDGE

The *Wasp* crosses the finish line. *(underwater)*

EXT. POND

The *Womrath* beaches itself on the bank next to the finish line.

EXT. BRIDGE

The crowd goes wild.

Stuart sails from under the bridge. The Victor!

>   A PARENT
>   Who is that mouse, anyway?

>   GEORGE
>   That's no mouse, that's my brother.

MUSIC OUT:
INT. LITTLE HOME – HALLWAY – NIGHT

The RELATIVES have returned.

A HUGE CHEER goes up as George and Stuart descend the stairs, in matching TUXEDOES. (George carries a SAILING TROPHY in his arms.) The entire Little family surge forward to congratulate them.

>   GEORGE AND STUART
>   Little hi, Little lo!

>   ALL THE LITTLES
>   Little hey, Little ho!

George and Stuart reach the bottom of the stairs.

>   CRENSHAW
>   You know what? This calls for a picture.

CUT TO:
INT. LIVING ROOM – NIGHT

Mr. and Mrs. Little hoist George and Stuart onto the coffee table to pose for the picture. Uncle Stretch grabs a camera.

Uncle Stretch hesitates.

>   MR. LITTLE
>   What's wrong?

>   STRETCH
>   It's just that . . . You four look great together.

The Littles grin as one, ear to ear.

>   STUART *(to no one)*
>   This is the happiest moment of my life. I feel ten inches tall . . . .

He looks to the camera, happier than he's ever felt in his whole life . . . flash, the picture is taken.

THE FRONT DOORBELL RINGS, and everyone turns. Mr. Little goes to open it . . . And every pair of eyes in here drops straight down:

TWO TINY FIGURES STAND IN THE DOORWAY.

They are REGINALD AND CAMILLE STOUT — a married pair of mice, in their 50s, formally dressed.

He was an adventurous little fellow and loved the feel of the breeze in his face and the cry of the gulls overhead and the heave of the great swell under him.

—E. B. WHITE, *STUART LITTLE*, 1945

REGINALD
Mr. Little?

The crowd parts. Mr. Little steps forward.

MR. LITTLE
Yes?

REGINALD
Down here. Very sorry to disturb you at your lovely abode.

CAMILLE
I hope we're not intruding.

REGINALD
My name's Reginald Stout. This is my wife Camille.

CAMILLE
An extreme pleasure.

REGINALD
We're looking for Stuart.

CAMILLE
Yup.

MR. LITTLE
Are you friends of his?

REGINALD
Well, not exactly.

MRS. LITTLE
Fellow yachtsmen?

REGINALD
Guess again . . .

CAMILLE
Reggie . . . just tell them.

REGINALD
We're his parents!

CAMILLE
Yep. That's right.

REGINALD
Hey, where is the little guy?

The place goes dead silent. On Stuart . . .

CUT TO:

INT. LIVING ROOM – NIGHT
On one side of a table sit the Littles (Stuart on the arm of Mr. Little's chair). Reginald and Camille stand on the table, opposite. A long, uncomfortable beat of silence passes:

John Dykstra on Shooting the Boats

The boat race sequence was shot in two separate places. The live-action scenes with the Little family at the edge of the pond and the beginning of the race were shot on a soundstage. The boats racing, once they pass under the bridge, was shot as a second unit in a one-million-gallon tank with a sixty-five-foot-tall backing. For the lighting to match the work from the first unit, the second-unit race scenes had to be shot under a "silk," which was a huge piece of cloth stretched over the top of the tank to soften the light. Our silk was more than an acre of cloth and had to be hoisted and reefed like a sail when the wind rose and fell. It was like being on a sailing ship.

The boats were real-scale models and the mechanical effects crew rigged tracks on the bottom of the tank to pull them through the maneuvers called for by the scene. Wave-making machines rolled the surface of the tank and the wind machines filled the sails of the boats and made ripples on the surface of the water.

We wanted the time we spent with Stuart in the race to be a little magical and bring us into his world, to experience the race from a mouse point of view. The sequence was photographed at a high camera speed, which would make the boats move in slow motion. The slow motion of the boats and the water made them look larger than they actually were. We also positioned the camera low over the water and close to the boats to capture a mouse POV feeling.

1. *Special-effects foreman Brent Bell rigging the cable for the boat track with Jim Girch and Eric Dressor.*

2. *The pond was filled with water and then dyed to both hide the tracks and to simulate the look of real New York City pond water.*

3. *Special-effects divers securing the boats to their tracks for a shot.*

94

. Josh Culp, a model maker from Thunderstone, repairs a stay line n the overscaled Wasp. This larger version of the boat, done one nd a half times the size of the original boat, was used in close-up hots to get depth of field.

7. On deck, second unit director and visual effects supervisor John Dykstra directs Eric Allard and second unit first assistant director Fred Roth. In the water (left to right): Jay Bartus, Paul Vigal, and Dick Anderson.

. Veteran special-effects diver Dick Anderson taking instructions hile placing a boat in the water.

SECOND UNIT SHOOT
11/15/98–1/2/99 AT PARAMOUNT

8. The film crew prepares to shoot the Wasp and the Womrath rounding the buoy. At left, the camera assistant holds the slate describing the shot, number, and take.

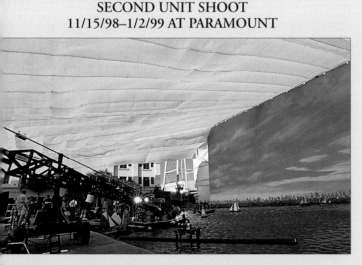

. Almost an acre of white silk was draped above the water to atch the soft light of the first-unit shoot on Stage 30. In the reground is a machine called a "wave maker."

9. Diver Jay Bartus stands by the overscale Womrath during insert (close-up) photography.

Model builder Timothy Huchthausen discusses the Wasp *rigging with divers Eric Dressor, Tony VanDenecker, and first unit special effects lead man William Aldridge. A fifty-five-foot super techno-crane extended over the pond to photograph the boats.*

REGINALD
(trying to decide what peanut to choose)
Mmmm . . . *(eating nuts)* Mmmm!
CRUNCH . . . mmm.

CAMILLE
Reggie! Stop it!

REGINALD
Oof! *(nervous titter)* Ahhem.

CAMILLE
It's so good to see you again, Stuart . . . There's so much we have to catch up on.

STUART
Why didn't you want me?

Camille starts to weep.

REGINALD
Stuart, it shames me to say this, but you weren't born into a prosperous home . . .

CAMILLE
That's right. We couldn't feed you, dear.

GEORGE
Couldn't feed him?! How much could he eat?!

MR. LITTLE
George, please.

Reginald SMACKS HIS LIPS.

CAMILLE
Letting you go was the toughest choice we ever made.

STUART
It was?

CAMILLE
Yes. But now we can be a family again!

REGINALD
Absolutely . . . Are these salted?

He inspects the peanuts in his hand and takes a bite.

REGINALD *(cont'd)*
Mmmm.

MRS. LITTLE
(do something)
Dear?

Mr. Little clears his throat. Then:

MR. LITTLE
Ah . . . yeah . . . George, Stuart, I think we need to talk to the Stouts alone.

Stuart just stares, in a daze. George gently picks him up, carrying him out.

GEORGE *(whispering:)*
Don't worry. Mom and Dad will take care of it.

The boys turn the corner.

MRS. LITTLE
Mr. and Mrs. Stout, I'm afraid there's been a mistake.

MR. LITTLE
Right!

MRS. LITTLE
Stuart can't leave with you. He's . . .

MR. LITTLE
. . . one of the family.

MRS. LITTLE
Exactly.

Reginald wipes the nut-crumbs from his mouth.

REGINALD
Mr. and Mrs. Little, you may feel like he's family, but he'll never really be family.

CAMILLE
You may not realize it, but I'm sure he does.

REGINALD
There's something you'll never be able to give him — because you're human — no offense . . .

CAMILLE
It's a place you'll never be able to fill.

Mrs. Little takes a sharp breath.

MRS. LITTLE
An empty space?

Beat. Neither couple says anything for a while.

Mr. and Mrs. Little don't reply; they're too shaken.

CUT TO:

INT. LIVING ROOM – NIGHT
Stuart's eyes are saucers. George's too. All the Little family members stand around the room looking uncomfortable.

"I will be happiest if people forget that Stuart is animated. He should be accepted as one of the lead actors in the film, along with Geena Davis and Hugh Laurie. There were hundreds of people involved in the creation of Stuart, all focused on making our contribution invisible. We all just want everyone to fall in love with Stuart Little."
—HENRY ANDERSON III, ANIMATION SUPERVISOR

Jonathan Lipnicki and Rob Minkoff.

STUART
Mom? Dad? You want me to leave?

MR. LITTLE
No.

MRS. LITTLE
Oh, dear, we just want what's best for you.

GEORGE
But Stuart lives here!

MR. LITTLE
George, come on. This is hard for all of us.

GEORGE
This stinks!

George storms out and slams the basement door.

STUART
I don't understand. I thought I was in a fairy tale . . .

REGINALD
Fairy tales are made-up stories, Stuart. This is real. This is about where you belong.

Camille comes up next to him.

CAMILLE
Please come home, Stuart. Your real home.

REGINALD
You're gonna love it, Son. We live on a golf course. We look right over the ninth fairway.

CAMILLE
It's beautiful.

REGINALD
Beautiful.

CUT TO:
EXT. LITTLE HOME – MOMENTS LATER
Reginald and Camille are standing out by the curb. Reginald is attempting to hail a CAB.

REGINALD *(whistles)*
Hey, taxi! Argh! What's a mouse have to do to get a cab in this city?

REVEAL Mr. and Mrs. Little on the front steps, watching, sadly. Stuart comes outside, carrying his little suitcase and dressed in his orphanage clothes.

STUART
You'll speak to George for me, won't you? I'd hate to say good-bye to a basement door.

MR. LITTLE
Of course.

Mrs. Little nods.

ANGLE ON REGINALD AND CAMILLE.

A cab has stopped.

REGINALD
Taxi . . . Taxi . . . Yo, yo . . . Taxi! Time to go, Stuart.

Stuart nods, desperate to stay. Then he braces himself.

STUART
Well . . . Good-bye.

Stuart says good-bye to the family. Mrs. Little kisses him.

MRS. LITTLE
We love you.

STUART
I . . . I love you, too, Mom. *(clears his throat)*

MRS. LITTLE.
Mr. Little carries him down the stairs.

REGINALD
Boy, that looks heavy. You need some help with that? . . . Camille?

Mr. and Mrs. Little are alone on the steps.

MRS. LITTLE
Frederick, let's do something!

MR. LITTLE
What?

MRS. LITTLE
Let's just make them . . . go away. We're bigger than they are. We'll say "Go! Shoo!" We'll scare their little whiskers off.

MR. LITTLE
Eleanor, you're not being rational.

MRS. LITTLE
Rational, shmational. Something about this is not right. I just know it!

MR. LITTLE
Look at them. They just . . . fit.

MRS. LITTLE
So what? I have shoes that fit and I hate them. As Stuart's mother I ought to . . .

DOUGLAS WICK ON CASTING

Casting the Littles was an incredibly challenging job. They needed to be an eccentric family, but the kind who made you secretly wish you were one of them. They needed to be the attractive side of eccentrics, the kind of people who always looked like they were having fun. If you saw them in the park, you'd want to be on their picnic blanket.

It was hard because we kept looking at actors who were eccentric in ways that would make you happier if they stayed on their side of the park. Or we looked at actors who were so mainstream, so ordinary, that there was no magic to them at all. We only began to get excited about the Littles when we focused on Geena Davis as the mom. Geena says the reason we chose her was because she had experience in working with other species, but the truth is that she has humanity and humor, she's very much her own person, and she doesn't quite seem like anyone else.

Then we had to decide who to cast opposite Geena as Mr. Little. We looked at every American actor, but we couldn't find anyone who, with Geena, seemed like a family. We needed the same kind of balance: attractive, witty, compelling, and eccentric. Then one day the head of Sony casting suggested Hugh Laurie, and he was just the perfect fit.

The challenge in casting the son, George, was that the kid is very dismissive and unhappy with his new brother for most of the movie, and without a very sympathetic actor in this part, we'd have a very big problem. Originally we wanted a ten-year-old, but Rob Minkoff asked us to consider Jonathan Lipnicki, even though he was only seven years old at the time. We'd seen Jonathan in *Jerry Maguire,* and he was magical. He has incredible screen presence and he seemed like a Little. So we gave Jonathan and Hugh similar glasses and we had our Little family.

Of course, our greatest casting challenge was the part of Stuart because we needed a mouse who had screen presence and could carry a movie. That's a short list. Our casting director suggested that perhaps Stuart should play himself. I must admit that I was quite dubious. But Stuart Little came into the office and I was genuinely surprised. He was totally right for the movie.

He was so kind and considerate. He was the type of guy who said hello to everyone when he came on the set in the morning. He never complained when the donuts were a little stale—not that he ate that much anyway.

He insisted on doing all his own stunts, even the real sweaty, backbreaking jumps. There's a scene where Stuart has to float on his suitcase and then jump down a drain, and he insisted on doing it himself. We were all really nervous. I thought maybe, if worse came to worst, I'd have an insurance claim but no movie. We tried to talk him into using a stunt mouse but he wouldn't have it. He did the scene very well, several times actually, and the good news is, he lived.

MR. LITTLE *(gently)*
But you're not. She is.

GEORGE (O.S.)
Stuart!

George bursts out the front door, and runs to Stuart.

GEORGE *(cont'd)*
Wait!

STUART
George!

They're both about to cry . . .

GEORGE
I want you to have this.

He puts the ROADSTER *(top up)* down onto the sidewalk. Stuart doesn't know what to say. Breaking the silence:

STUART
Ah, George . . . not the roadster, George. You love this car. I couldn't.

GEORGE
I want you to.

The brothers eye each other.

STUART
Thanks, George . . .

GEORGE
I wish you didn't have to go. I'm gonna miss you.

STUART
I'll miss you, too, George.

Reginald runs his hand over the Roadster as he gets behind the wheel.

The cab leaves.

Stuart climbs in back, with his tiny suitcases now packed with the clothes Mrs. Little had bought for him.

The car starts up and starts to drive away down the sidewalk. Stuart presses his face against the back window and manages a tiny wave.

The Littles sadly wave good-bye.

George turns and runs into the house, slamming the door. Then:

SNOWBELL (O.S.)
Meow?

THE STOUTS

A BRIEF BIOGRAPHY BY HENRY ANDERSON III

The Stouts, Reginald and Camille, were not part of the E. B. White book. They were created specifically for the film to help further the plot. As original creations, there was no background information on them to help guide the animators and the artists. Animation Supervisor Henry Anderson III wrote the following "biography" of the Stouts to help his team of animators and himself to visualize the characters.

A middle-aged couple, the Stouts have been together for many years. They have spent a great deal of time running from creditors, wronged business associates, cats, etcetera, as a result of Reginald's many scams.

Despite their life, Reginald is always able to convince Camille that everything is under control, that it is all working according to plan, and, most important, that he is a success in his various business ventures. Even though they've lived on the run, they were enjoying a welcome period of stability before they were cornered on the ninth hole and roped into kidnapping Stuart.

CAMILLE
- Grew up a poor mouse on the wrong side of the tracks.
- Met "Reggie" while working as a cocktail waitress, and he has provided the only decent home she's ever known.
- She thinks he has "class."
- She is very emotional and, though sort of dippy, she has a good heart.
- Likes children, though she can't have any herself.
- She has convinced herself that Stuart can become their adopted son.
- Enjoys playing Stuart's mom to the extent that she really is heartbroken when she realizes they have to turn him over to the cats. At this point, her tears are real.

REGINALD
- A self-made mouse and a hustler.
- Always has one scheme or another going to keep his head above water.
- Knows every other hustler in town.
- No formal education, can't even read.
- Tries to convince his friends that he was raised in a privileged home. (Note: Camille believes this.)
- Attempts to appear sophisticated at all times.
- Has a genuine regard for Camille.
- Even though he is brusque with Camille, he'd do anything for her.
- She really is the best thing that ever happened to him.
- Even though he is primarily looking out for himself, he, like Camille, has a good heart and could never really harm anyone.

Early concept drawings of the Stouts by Thor Freudenthal.

They look down to find Snowbell, at the base of the stoop. Mr. Little walks down the steps, scoops up the cat, and enters the house again without a word . . .

CUT TO:
TRAVELING —

REGINALD/CAMILLE *(singing).*

EXT. – FUNLAND – NIGHT —The car rolls beneath a sign that says "Funland." This is an abandoned amusement park.

EXT. "9TH FAIRWAY" – CONTINUING
The Roadster drives along a thin stretch of ASTROTURF with short concrete curbs on either side . . . until we realize that we're in the middle of a MINIATURE GOLF HOLE.

REGINALD
So here we are, Stuie . . . Home sweet home. Ain't it grand?

CAMILLE
You should've seen this place before it was condemned as a safety hazard.

REGINALD
Oh yeah, those were the days. Kids running around, dropping little bits of food everywhere. Those miniature golf pencils to gnaw on.

CAMILLE
It was paradise.

REGINALD
Paradise.

And at the edge of it is the "Stout" castle Reginald promised. (When this course was in business, golf balls used to spit out of its bottom.)

We TRACK WITH STUART as he cranes his neck, eyeing his new surroundings. A lump sticks in his throat.

REGINALD
But don't worry, son. We'll fix it up.

CUT TO:
EXT. "STOUT CASTLE" – MOMENTS LATER (NIGHT)
Pan over exterior of Stout Castle.

REGINALD (V.O.)
I bet you're feeling pretty lucky, finding your parents, coming to live in a castle on a golf course all in the same day. I know what you're thinking:

How can I ever repay them? Relax, we'll talk about that in the morning.

CAMILLE
Your new bedroom, Stuart.

REGINALD
We hope you like it.

Stuart sets his suitcase down on the bed.

REGINALD *(cont'd)*
Well good night, sleep tight, don't let the bedbugs bite. *(stops)* I'm serious about the bedbugs, keep an eye open.

(exits)

With that, he's gone. Stuart just stands there, alone in his brand-new room.

Stuart looks out the attic window; from here he can see that AstroTurf fairway, and most of the rest of the ABANDONED COURSE — (decrepit, lifeless.)

. . . but beyond the golf course he can see Manhattan's Skyline, twinkling. It's glorious.

"Real life is only one kind of life—there is also the life of the imagination. And although my stories are imaginary, I like to think that there is some truth to them, too—truth about the way people and animals feel and think and act."

—E. B. WHITE

CUT TO:

INT. LAUNDRY ROOM – DAY

Mrs. Little is folding laundry. She finds one of Stuart's little T-shirts.

She starts to cry.

INT. LITTLE HOME – LIVING ROOM – AFTERNOON

Mrs. Little leads MRS. KEEPER, into the room.

> MRS. LITTLE
> It's very kind of you to come and check on us like this.

> MRS. KEEPER
> Actually, I had something to tell you. But, first, how are things going?

> MRS. LITTLE
> It's been difficult.

> MRS. KEEPER
> Difficult?

> MRS. LITTLE
> Very difficult.

> MRS. KEEPER
> Very difficult?

Mr. Little enters with beverages.

> MR. LITTLE
> Worse.

> MRS. KEEPER
> Worse than very difficult?

> MRS. LITTLE
> Yes, it's been almost . . .

> MR. LITTLE
> Unbearable.

> MRS. LITTLE
> Just the word I was looking for.

MRS. KEEPER shakes her head, concerned.

> MRS. KEEPER
> Maybe this isn't a good time then. I'm afraid I have some . . . uh . . . news.

> MRS. LITTLE
> What type of news?

HUGH LAURIE ON COSTARRING WITH STUART

*S*tuart is a terrific performer and we're all kind of in awe of him. At the same time, we just wish he wouldn't push to the front of the line at the craft services and stuff like that. I don't know whether the stardom thing has gone to his head or something. He's got a very, very big head. Well, I say a big head even though relative to a human being, it's quite a small head, but for a mouse, it's a big head.

The first thing he said to me when we met was, "Stay out of my light," and we weren't even on the set. We were in an elevator. Actually, I don't blame him for it. There's not a lot of light down there and he's got to scoop it up where he can find it. He's got to look out for himself.

Height jokes were not well received the first week. He made it pretty clear that height or whiskers or anything to do with cheese was not funny. We had a couple of good cheese jokes but they had to go; he wasn't having them. But, again, I can't really blame him for that as long as he delivers on the screen, which he does and it's gold. A cheesy kind of gold, but it's gold.

There's something very Brando-ish about Stuart. Or maybe there's something mousey about Brando—I don't know who was there first so it's hard to say. You never really know, people take influences from all over the place.

MRS. KEEPER (*deep breath*)
They had an accident . . .

MRS. LITTLE
Who?

MRS. KEEPER
Stuart's parents.

Snowbell looks up.

SNOWBELL (*concerned*)
Hmmm.

MR. LITTLE
Oh my goodness? Are they all right?

MRS. KEEPER
No. They didn't make it.

MRS. LITTLE
Oh my.

MR. LITTLE
What happened?

MRS. KEEPER
Apparently, they were grocery shopping . . .
Canned food aisle. There was an unsteady
pyramid of cans. It collapsed.

MRS. KEEPER
It took three bag boys to dig them out. They had to
identify them by their dental records.

MRS. LITTLE
Oh, how horrible!

MRS. KEEPER
Creamed mushroom soup . . . Two for one sale . . .
That's a very heavy soup.

MRS. LITTLE
How's Stuart taking it?

MRS. KEEPER
He doesn't know.

MR. LITTLE
You mean no one's told him?

MRS. KEEPER
Does he *have* to know?

MR. LITTLE
Well in six months after they don't come back from shopping, isn't he going to wonder where they went?

MRS. KEEPER
But they've been gone for years.

MRS. LITTLE
Years? How is that possible?

MRS. KEEPER
Because . . . they died! Years ago. Which part is confusing you?

MRS. LITTLE
Stuart's parents came and took him away three days ago.

MRS. KEEPER
Three days ago . . . Stuart's parents died in a tragic Creamed Mushroom Soup incident years ago. I just told you.

MRS. KEEPER nods "Yes" slowly. All breathing stops.

MRS. LITTLE
Dear, we have to take this up with the police.

Snowbell hops off Mrs. Little's lap and goes out of the room.

CUT TO:
EXT. LITTLE HOUSE – NIGHT – ESTABLISHING
A police car pulls up in front of the Littles' brownstone.

INT. LITTLE HOME – NIGHT
Mr. and Mrs. Little OPEN the FRONT DOOR REVEALING TWO PLAINCLOTHES DETECTIVES.

SHERMAN
Mrs. Little, I'm Detective Sherman, this is my partner, Detective Allen. We understand your son is missing. *(they flash badges)*

MR. LITTLE *(showing them in)*
Thank you for coming.

They all enter the living room.

EXT. ALLEY
Snowbell and Monty are speaking to Red and his "boys."

THE MAN WITH THE MOVES: BILL IRWIN

The multitalented Bill Irwin was hired at the start of production to help animators inspire a library of movements and poses for Stuart Little. "Bill is a gifted, inspirational, eccentric dancer, comic, and mime artist," says Animation Supervisor Henry Anderson. "We wanted to instill something of Bill's special talent in the way Stuart moved. Stuart needed to communicate without saying a word, which is what Bill is so good at doing. We spent several days working with him to form a library of motions and mannerisms that we could reference throughout the production."

Irwin was videotaped performing many of the tasks that Stuart would need to act out in the film, such as walking while carrying a heavy suitcase or falling down. Irwin posed in many stances that would eventually be incorporated into Stuart's overall look.

Like silent-film star Buster Keaton, another inspiration for Stuart, Irwin uses physical movement to show us how the character thinks and reacts to situations. The movements are exaggerated for effect. For example, when walking, for dramatic effect the feet are extended out much farther than an average step.

JEROME CHEN ON CREATING THE DIGITAL MOVIE STAR

Visual effects artists have an old credo: The effect should support the story. The challenge of Stuart Little was both daunting and enticing: The lead character could be realized only through special visual effects. As the lead, Stuart had to be more than a sustained illusion meant to enhance the story; he needed to be engaging and convincing enough to draw the audience into the very heart and soul of the film.

The initial phase of Stuart's creation had very traditional roots. Artists sketched him on paper, offering various styles of his fur and features. Costume designers drew up his wardrobe, providing him with attire for his adventures: an orphanage uniform, a party suit, a sweater and khakis, even a sailor outfit. As these sketches worked their way through the approval circles, it was difficult to tell that the actor in question was not flesh and blood. In the computer, we escalated his design process and fully realized him on film.

A core group of computer graphics artists took Stuart and dissected him into a series of complex design processes. Teams were formed to focus on the various aspects that would ultimately provide him with his realism: his skin, fur, and clothes. These artists dealt with Stuart at his very finest level of detail, down to the texture and wetness of his nose and even the reflectivity of his eyes. Digital sculptors used 3-D modeling software to create a virtual library of dozens of Stuart's facial expressions, which would form the range of his performance. Another team built Stuart's body and his digital skeleton, programming the kinematics of his movements. Eventually we had a full working figure of a Stuart ready to be animated and rendered.

The next stage of his development was the most important, because it was time to consider how he should look in the film reality established by the cinematographer of the film, Guillermo Navarro. Our approach to Stuart's lighting was no different than how Guillermo lit Geena Davis: We treated him as a movie star. Computer graphic 3-D lighting tools are primitive when compared to what is available to a live-action cinematographer, so a team of technical artists was tasked to create a suite of more sophisticated lighting software to help us attain our visual goal. These tools enabled us to fully realize Stuart, rendering him with soft key-to-fill ratios and accent rim lights to set off highlight glints on the edges of his fur. This lighting scheme established Stuart's realism because it had the same sense of illumination as the actors. We worked very hard to take Stuart's level of lighting beyond that of mere integration with the live-action background plate; we wanted him to appear to be lit with the care that any cinematographer lavishes on his star.

The lead visual effects team (from left), Jay Redd, Jim Berney, Jerome Chen, and Scott Stokdyk, reviewing some of the numerous drawings and maquettes of Stuart Little.

Every day, the visual effects team reviewed their progress at the computer terminals of the artists who were meticulously creating Stuart's fur and clothing. At workstations through-out Imageworks, digital artists went through the film, literally frame by frame, electronically applying light, shadows, and shading with Vermeer-like precision that made Stuart pop as a three-dimensional character. "It has the mentality of painting, where the image is created layer by layer," says Jerome Chen, himself an artist by training, of this very exacting process.

SNOWBELL
They know about the Stouts! They know about the Stouts! The jig is up. What're we going to do?

MONTY
Hey, get ahold of yourself. What're you talking about?

SNOWBELL
This is very . . . I'm in big . . . I'm in deep poopy doo.

MONTY
Calm down. Calm down. Don't get your fur in a bunch. All we need is a new plan.

SMOKEY
We do what we should've done in the first place. We scratch him out.

MONTY
Scratch him out?

SNOWBELL
But Smokey . . . The police are involved! I don't

want to get kicked out of my house. I'm not a street cat, I'm a house cat. I don't want to lose my little furry basket, my little tinkle ball I push across the floor with my nose.

MONTY
Snow, buddy, pull yourself together.

SMOKEY
It's settled. *(to his boys)* Stuart Little gets scratched tonight . . .

INT. DINING ROOM – A MOMENT LATER
Detective Allen continues into the living room, where the other detectives are picking out the peanuts from the dish with a tweezer and sealing them in a plastic bag, snapping photos, dusting for prints [or whatever exact business is determined by director].

Detective Sherman is in the living room, on the phone. He hangs up and approaches Mrs. Little and Mr. Little.

DETECTIVE SHERMAN *(into phone)*
Okay . . . very good.

He hangs up.

DETECTIVE SHERMAN *(cont'd)*
Mr. and Mrs. Little, you'll have to come downtown.

INT. POLICE STATION

We see Sherman and Mr. and Mrs. Little looking straight ahead.

"Oh, fish feathers!" said Stuart. "Size has nothing to do with it. It's temperament and ability that count."
—E. B. WHITE, *STUART LITTLE*, 1945

SHERMAN
Turn to the left.

ANGLE ON A LINE-UP

Of mice. Shifty-looking mice. Reluctantly they turn.

ANGLE ON SHERMAN AND THE LITTLES

SHERMAN *(cont'd)*
Anything?

The Littles shake their heads.

MR. LITTLE
No.

SHERMAN
Next group.

INT. POLICE STATION
The Littles are at Sherman's desk.

MR. LITTLE
Detective Sherman, what are the chances of seeing Stuart again?

SHERMAN
You want it straight?

Mr. and Mrs. Little look at each other. Then . . .

MR. LITTLE
No.

MRS. LITTLE
Absolutely not.

SHERMAN
Well, in that case, Stuart's probably at home right now waiting for you.

The Littles look at each other again. Then . . .

MR. LITTLE
Maybe we should hear it a little straighter than that.

SHERMAN
Okay . . . In a case like this if the kidnappers have not called by now, then they're not interested in money.

MR. LITTLE
What are they interested in?

DETECTIVE ALLEN
Kicks.

SHERMAN
Exactly. It's my guess these two sickos are on some kind of a cross-country mouse-killing spree.

MRS. LITTLE
Oh no!

MR. LITTLE *(to Sherman)*
Well, thank you.

They start to go, but Sherman keeps going.

SHERMAN
Yeah . . . you can kiss this boy good-bye.

MR. LITTLE
Thank you, Detective.

SHERMAN
It's over. The things I've seen. *(calls)* Phil, where's that book on the grisly photos? *(back to the Littles)* Believe me, you don't want to see this.

MR. LITTLE
Ah . . . uh . . . no, well.

They start to leave again.

Jon Polito and Jim Doughan as the two detectives on the case for Stuart.

"One of the greatest challenges of this movie was shooting the scenes with the cats. As actors, cats tend not to take direction very well. They don't always find their mark and they rarely do what you tell them to do. This meant we needed to shoot a lot of film for each scene. In the final scene with the cats, we shot more than eighty thousand feet of film for just four minutes of screen time."

—ROB MINKOFF, DIRECTOR

SHERMAN *(cont'd)*
It'll only take a second. *(opening the book)* Whew!! Right off the bat, look at this one. This one kept me awake for weeks.

He holds it up to them.

We can't see it but the Littles react with DISGUST.

MR. AND MRS. LITTLE
Oh!

CUT TO:
EXT. "STOUT HOUSE" – CASTLE – NIGHT

CAMILLE
What did they want?

REGINALD
Where's the boy?

CAMILLE
Oh no.

AS WE PUSH IN ON Stuart's turret:

REGINALD (V.O.)
Stuart, wake up. Get dressed.

STUART (V.O.)
Why?

Pause.

REGINALD (V.O.)
We're taking you for a ride.

STUART (V.O.)
Where are we going?

Now we can see the characters in the window.

REGINALD (V.O.)
Some friends of ours have gathered just to meet you.

STUART
A gathering? What should I wear?

REGINALD
It doesn't matter. Wear anything.

STUART
Is it formal?

REGINALD
Just put something on.

WE HEAR A SOB.

STUART (V.O.)
Why is Mom crying?

TRUE STATISTICS

During the shooting of the cat scenes, production used:

—9,360 cans of cat food
—3,000 pounds of kitty litter
—4 kilos of catnip

INTRODUCING STUFFY

During the shooting of the live action, filmmakers had to make a space in every shot for Stuart, who would later be composited. The continuity of the film and the believability of the character demanded that, even when the actors were talking to empty space, they were looking at the exact space where Stuart would eventually exist.

To help the cameramen and the actors visualize their costar, a series of Stuart stand-ins were created. Many different versions of the doll-like Stuart were used throughout the filming, including one that was known as Stuart-on-a-stick. Collectively known as "Stuffy," the stuffed mouse became the film's punching bag. "He had all sorts of nasty jokes played on him," says Dykstra.

Though Stuffy performed admirably as Stuart's stand-in during rehearsals and in setting up the shots, he was removed when the cameras began to roll. In his place, during the actual shots, a red laser dot, calibrated to the camera shutter, functioned as a marker for Stuart's position in the scene. The actors learned to "love the dot" in place of Stuart.

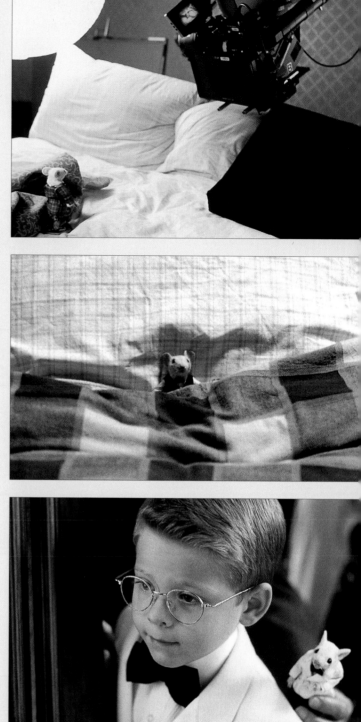

Wanna-be performer Stuffy acting as the stand-in for Stuart in several scenes from the movie: in the orphanage when Stuart first meets the Littles (left), in bed on Stuart's first night home when he is both kissed good night by Geena Davis and then terrified by Snowbell, and when the Stouts ruin the Little family celebration.

Animation Supervisor Henry Anderson III on the Central Park set during the shooting of the scene in which Stuart drops the boat's remote control. Anderson holds a version of Stuffy that is attached to a stick to show the actors where Stuart will move in the scene. The nickname for this particular Stuffy was "Rod Stuart."

EXT. STOUT CASTLE – NIGHT – LATER
Camille is still crying as they exit the castle and head for the roadster.

STUART
Mom, I'm not angry at you for putting me up for adoption. And now that I'm a Stout again, I'll always be here to take care of you. *(Camille cries louder)* Because that's what families do, Mom. They take care of each other.

Camille, suddenly cries even louder then whacks Reginald over the head with her purse.

REGINALD
Ow!

CAMILLE
Tell him the truth!

EXT. STOUT CASTLE – NIGHT – LATER
The roadster is parked.

STUART
You made a deal with a cat?

REGINALD
He had us cornered! At the bottom of a cup on the 5th hole!

CAMILLE
It was curtains!

STUART
So you agreed to pose as my parents?

REGINALD
Yes.

STUART
You lied and cheated?

REGINALD AND CAMILLE *(ashamed)*
Yes.

STUART
You took me away from the Littles just when we were all so happy?

REGINALD AND CAMILLE *(breaking)*
Yes.

A beat.

STUART
That's wonderful!

Pause.

REGINALD
I think you missed something. Let me go over it again.

STUART
That's why I've been feeling so sad! That's why I keep thinking of them! I'm not a Stout! I'm a Little! I'm Stuart Little! I'm Stuart Little!

That was so loud that Reginald had to cover Stuart's mouth.

REGINALD
Stuart, please, you have to listen to us. The cats have decided you're too risky to keep around anymore. They ordered us to hand you over to them! As your fake father, I order you to run.

STUART
I'll go home!

REGINALD
Home?! No, no, that's miles from here. And it's dark out. And every cat in the city is looking for you.

CAMILLE
Besides, you could get lost.

ROB MINKOFF ON VOICE-OVERS

When we cast for voice-overs, we are looking for a distinctive voice that has a presence and can convey character with only sound. Some actors excel at voice-overs because they deliver a performance with just their voice.

The actor for Stuart himself was one of the most difficult to cast. The actor needed a certain soulfulness, and though he was only a nine-year-old child, he needed to act as an older mentor for George. Michael J. Fox was the perfect choice from the very start. He seemed to have the right kind of personality for Stuart—very positive, sincere, and winning, yet with an edge. His voice projects adult attitude with a youthful quality and energy. This is a very rare combination.

Still, it was a hard job for Michael, who is really much more streetwise than the character and has a sharp, sarcastic wit. We were constantly trying to find a way to bring some humor and attitude to Stuart without compromising his character. My challenge was to make Stuart both sweet and interesting. The easiest place to go with this kind of character is "cute," but that can also become really annoying if you take cuteness too far.

Nathan Lane, who plays Snowbell, has one of the strongest voices of any actor. His delivery has an energy and a rhythm that is a lot like music. With just his voice, Nathan makes an indelible imprint on the film.

Steve Zahn plays Monty, who I thought of as the Eddie Haskell of cats. For Smokey we needed a New York tough cat with a voice to match. Chazz Palminteri, who plays the quintessential tough guy, was perfect for this role. And of course the Stouts are played brilliantly by Jennifer Tilly and Bruno Kirby. Just by listening to Jennifer and Bruno speak their first lines, you get an instant sense of what these characters are all about.

STUART
No, no I can't! Every Little in the world can find the Little house.

In the distance, we hear a loud wail: "MEOWWW!!!!!" They all know what that sound means.

SMASH CUT TO:

EXT. SAME SPOT – A MOMENT LATER
The wheels of the ROADSTER kick up dust.

STUART *(over his shoulder)*
Good-bye, Fake Father! Good-bye, Fake Mother!

CAMILLE
Good-bye, Fake Son!

REGINALD
Good-bye, Stuart.

They're left alone.

CAMILLE
I'm gonna miss that boy.

REGINALD
I'm gonna miss that car.

EXT./INT. LITTLE HOME – NIGHT
Mr. and Mrs. Little are returning home from the police station. They pause at the door.

Actor Steve Zahn and director Rob Minkoff in the sound studio. Zahn voiced the part of Monty, Snowbell's best buddy, who Minkoff describes as "the Eddie Haskell of cats."

MRS. LITTLE
George?

MR. LITTLE
I think we have to . . .

MRS. LITTLE
. . . tell him.

MR. LITTLE
Yeah.

Mr. and Mrs. Little enter. CAMERA MOVES BEHIND THEM, over their shoulders, as they see the house is in a total frenzy. The entire Little clan is there, making posters, manning the phones, etc. A beehive of activity.

MRS. CRENSHAW *(on the phone)*
627 5th Avenue. I need three cabs.

GEORGE
WHO HAS THE GLUE!?!

UNCLE CRENSHAW
I'm the glue man.

MR. LITTLE
What's going on?

BEATRICE
We're making posters.

UNCLE STRETCH
We're gonna put them up all over the city.

Beatrice holds up a poster. Under the heading "MISSING" is a description of Stuart.

EDGAR
That's right. They describe Stuart and offer a reward if anyone finds him.

UNCLE CRENSHAW
Isn't it wonderful. It was all George's idea.

MR. LITTLE
George.

GEORGE
Never stop trying, right Dad?

MR. LITTLE *(softly)*
Listen . . . I'm afraid this isn't going to work.

GEORGE
Why not?

Jon Polito, Jim Doughan (background), Geena Davis, and Hugh Laurie.

Mrs. Little shoots him a reproachful look. He considers a Beat . . .

MR. LITTLE *(cont'd) (energetically)*
Because there's no picture. We need a picture of Stuart.

MRS. LITTLE
The family photo!

EXT. BROOKLYN BRIDGE
Stuart drives toward Manhattan.

EXT. ALLEY
Cats screech the news across the city.

LUCKY
Smokey. Hey Smokey.

SMOKEY
Keep it down.

LUCKY
Hey, it's me, Lucky. I just heard from the Brooklyn cats. Bad news . . . the Stouts squealed.

SMOKEY
This is what I get for trusting mice.

LUCKY
The kid's on his way home. What do we do?

JOHN DYKSTRA ON VISUAL EFFECTS

Whether you paint in oil or watercolor, or whether you create images on a computer screen, it's all the same kind of creative thinking. Your mind has to be capable of going beyond the bounds of the medium to bring in ideas from other environments. If you limit yourself to what the computer can do, then you will always be creating "computer art." When you incorporate ideas from other areas, then you can transcend that barrier.

I love film, but it is limited. Whether the problem is in the area of storytelling or the creation of something visual or technical, there is a finite number of solutions with film. The advent of the electronic medium has allowed us to expand what can be accomplished. There's really no limitation. If you had the time and money, you could create something that was completely outside the realm of corporeal storytelling. You could make 3-D images or 4-D images. This is truly a magic pencil.

From a visual effects point of view, the challenge of *Stuart Little* was to create a photo-realistic, computer-generated, furry, talking, leading man—or, should I say, a mouse with a very stylish wardrobe? Stuart has to be real both emotionally and intellectually for the story to reach its full potential. The animation had to express a complete range of human emotion with Stuart's face and body language. Stuart had to vocalize human words without his mouse's mouth becoming a cartoon. For the emotion of the animation to complement the emotional performances of the live actors, Stuart had to be intellectually real. We have all seen mice. We know how they move and how light reacts in their fur. We also know that they don't generally walk erect and wear clothes. Stuart's fur had to react to the light and physics of the real world. His clothing had to have texture, drape, and move like real clothing. The fur and clothing had to be blown by the wind and drenched by water, all under the tight scrutiny of the camera lens, which goes from very wide shots where Stuart is a "dot on the screen" to the extreme close-up where we can actually see the world reflected in his shiny black eyes. The audience must believe that we could have taught a real mouse to act and wear clothes. They need to believe that when the director yells "Cut," Stuart walks off the set along with Hugh and Geena and goes to his trailer to study his lines for the next scene. The scope of the work is huge and very cutting edge. We are going to make a movie star.

Since *Star Wars,* visual effects have undergone a complete and total rebirth. The computer is the tool responsible for this. The ability to create images one pixel at a time has provided the artists and technicians with what I consider to be an embarrassment of riches. Now the only limitation is the artist's imagination.

The computer is, however, only a tool. Diversity is not inherent in computers. They tend to break things down into the smallest component pieces, and, as a result, when you build from one pixel at a time, you start with simple things. Computers can model simple objects very well, but if you make a character of simple objects, they tend to look like a Tinkertoy as opposed to an organic object that contains huge variations of brightness, texture, and reflectivity. These variations are what give the viewer the subliminal clues as to the reality of an object. It is our attention to all these variations that makes Stuart seem real on the screen.

Senior Visual Effects Supervisor and Second Unit Director John Dykstra.

The volume of the mouse or the volume of anything made in a computer is defined by points in space. The points in space are connected by lines. The shapes made by those lines are called "polygons." If you fill in these shapes, sort of like coloring inside the lines, you get what's called the hardware-shaded object, which has a very limited range of lighting possibilities and color but gives you the volume as a closed structure.

The next step is a huge calculation that adds all of these subtleties: the business of the clothes, the color, the way the fur works, or even such details as what is reflected in the character's eyes. All of these small components contribute to creating the reality of the character in the real world. Accuracy is important. For example, we photographed the live-action set and used that image as a reflection in the character's eye, the way the surface of a real eye would reflect the real world.

Stuart Little is a great collaborative effort. There are hundreds of people working on Rob's vision. We've taken a lot of first steps here and they are very promising. The real test of whether we've succeeded or not is if the audience believes the characters are real.

SMOKEY
All right, get the gang together. If the mouse wants to get home, he's gotta come this way, right? And when he does, we'll have ourselves a picnic.

LUCKY
Oh, great. I'll bring herring.

SMOKEY
Shut up. Not that kind of picnic. All right, let's go.

EXT. CENTRAL PARK SOUTH – LATER NIGHT
Stuart turns the roadster into Central Park. He passes beneath the gate, a tiny traveler on the path into the dark expanse of the park.

CUT TO:
EXT. CENTRAL PARK – DRIVING – MOMENTS LATER
The moonlit silhouettes of trees glide by above him as the car passes beneath spooky shadows cast onto the footpath.

EXT. CENTRAL PARK – PATH JUNCTION
The roadster crests a rise and rolls to a stop. Stuart gets out, walks toward:

STUART'S P. O. V. – THE FORK IN THE PATH

STUART
Hmm . . . which way?

Around him, we hear the sound of something ominous . . .

Sounds like claws on pavement. Cat claws . . . He hears them. Cat shadows brush across Stuart and he turns a fraction of a second too late to see them.

A spooked Stuart edges toward his car. Suddenly a cat's paw appears before him.

SMOKEY
How ya' doin'? You must be Stuart.

STUART
Actually . . . no. But, I'll go get him for you.

RED
What's your hurry, Murray?

LUCKY
Yeah . . . Where you going, Murray . . . Stuart— What's his name?

Stuart's tires squeal as the car rockets away from the cats.

THE ANIMATION TEAM

To bring Stuart to life, a team of thirty computer graphics animators was assembled to work with Animation Supervisor Henry Anderson III. This team came primarily from three sources: the animators already in Sony Imageworks Digital Character Group (DCG), an extensive hiring search for animators from outside the studio, and through an open "animation audition" that Anderson held within the company.

In the audition, applicants were given the Stuart model, a simple room environment, and three props: a matchstick, a button, and a thimble. They had free rein to animate Stuart and to use these props in any way they wanted to. The only direction was that the scene that they created show personality and that it be at least ten seconds in length. The deadline for submission was two weeks.

Many people with little or no feature-character animation experience decided to apply—some were employees of Imageworks from other departments—and a few found positions in the DCG. Todd Pilger, for example, was primarily a technical director working on setting up the Stuart model for the film. He managed to create a minute-long piece (a remarkable amount of footage for a two-week deadline) of Stuart climbing the walls, trying frantically to get out of the room. It garnered Todd a position on the team.

Since Anderson had never worked with the majority of animators at Imageworks, even they were given the audition assignment to give him a better idea of their strengths and weaknesses, and what type of scenes they liked to do.

Stuart slams the door closed. THREE STREET CATS have him boxed in. They explode toward him at once, from several angles.

Stuart jams the car into gear and slams the accelerator to the floor. The tires spin, smoking. But instead of shooting forward the Roadster rockets away in reverse. The cats are almost as surprised as Stuart when he slips between them.

EXT. CENTRAL PARK – RAVINE

The Roadster flies off the edge of the path through the bushes and down a hill, backward, with the cats in hot pursuit. Stuart turns, the car skidding backward toward a gap in the bushes. The gap is at the top of a ledge and the Roadster is launched, doing a 180-degree bootleg turn in the air.

The cats leap from the ledge right on the Roadster's tail.

The Roadster lands facing forward in the bottom of a ravine slowing from the impact. The tires spin and bite, and the car rockets forward. The cats land in the same spot a split second later.

INT. PARK DRAINAGE CULVERT

The car continues down the ravine and directly into a drainage culvert. The headlights illuminate the tunnel as Stuart races along inches in front of the cats.

Two cats bear down on him and one SWIPES AT HIM with a razor-sharp claw. Stuart swerves right barely avoiding the blow. The car slides around a pile of debris, Stuart sees a clear shot to the end of the tube.

STUART'S P.O.V. – THE CULVERT

THREE MORE CATS leap into the culvert from ABOVE, blocking his way. (They dropped in through a drain opening.)

Stuart jerks the wheel to the left. The little car's speed carries it up the wall, looping along the top of the tube

Animators often look in the mirror when they are working on facial expressions. Here animator Delio Tramontozzi examines his own mouth to help him capture and define an emotional response for Stuart.

Anderson says that the submissions were varied and were often remarkable. In addition to demonstrating the skill and imagination of the animator, the tests helped Anderson allocate the workload. "We cast animators for their strengths," he says, "like casting actors for a live-action film. This test helped show me the skill level of the crew, as well as where everyone's interest lay. Some animators did tests of great subtlety, while others went much broader and had Stuart jumping and dancing around the room."

In giving assignments to the animators, Anderson divided up the shots based on their action. Some required a high level of facial animation, others were running shots, or walking shots, or stunt performances such as jumping or climbing. Some animators were given Stuart's subtler scenes. "There's a scene in the movie where Stuart sits in George's toy roadster and says something to the effect that this is the first time he feels like he fits in," remembers Anderson. "We gave that scene to Pepe Valencia, whose work has a great sensitivity and a gentle quality. Pepe animated Stuart running his hand along the car door as he struggles for the words to express his feelings. It's very communicative and it fits the moment perfectly."

The mark of a great animator, according to Anderson, is not so much the ability to draw or use a computer, though it helps to have these skills. "The best animators know how to act," says Anderson. "They are able to get inside the character and really bring that character to life. It requires a great deal of ability to take a lifeless computer model and create a complex emotional performance using only the two primary elements of animation: pose and timing."

and over the heads of the cats that were blocking his path.

The end of the culvert is coming up too fast for Stuart to stop.

INT. STORM DRAIN CISTERN
The car HURLS out of the culvert opening and plummets toward the water below.

The car makes a BIG SPLASH. All is quiet for a moment.

> CATS
> Wow. Did you see that? He is one wet cat. Forget about it. It's all over. He's gone. That's the end of that one. Yeah, right.

STUART'S SUITCASE POPS UP right next to him and he climbs onboard. Balancing precariously on the unstable raft, the water carries him toward the MAIN DRAIN opening at the other end of the cistern.

The cats stand frustrated in the culvert opening, unwilling to make the jump into the water. Stuart waves good-bye as his suitcase moves into the darkness of the main drain.

> *"Stuart is pretty erudite for a mouse of so few years. He is compassionate. He's the kind of movie star that once you've seen him on screen, you'd like to meet him in person. He's worldly and unique in the way that only an animal adopted into human society can be, because he carries genetic material that we don't. He's smart. He's honest and he's fast. What I am not telling anyone is that there are, in fact, mice who wear clothes and talk. You know, that Area 51 Project out in the desert. These aliens are mice who wear clothes and talk, but you won't tell anyone, right?"*
>
> —JOHN DYKSTRA, SENIOR VISUAL EFFECTS SUPERVISOR AND SECOND UNIT DIRECTOR

Drawing by Thor Freudenthal.

> CATS *(cont'd)*
> Hey, Smokey! There he is. I see the suitcase. Hey, you think that's our mouse? Get him. I ain't goin' in. Come on, Smokey, it ain't my turn.

INT. MAIN DRAIN
Stuart stops waving as a low RUMBLING echo begins to surround him. He strains to see the source of the growing roar. Just ahead is a GRATING lit by a soft glow from above. Below that grating is the source of all the noise, a SPILLWAY that drops into blackness. To Stuart it sounds like Niagara Falls.

Stuart has no choice. He positions himself and LEAPS just before his suitcase drops into the misty blackness. Stuart lands on the grating and grabs tightly to the bars.

EXT. LITTLE HOME
The family all exit the house, carrying posters.

> MR. LITTLE
> Crenshaw, Tina, Uncle Stretch . . . you go uptown. Cover as many streets as you can. Edgar, Beatrice, Spencer . . . you take downtown — every side street and back alley. Estelle, you better go with them.

> GEORGE
> Where do I go?

> MRS. LITTLE
> You'll come with us. We're going to circle the park.

They all disperse excitedly. The street is quiet for a moment.

WE PUSH IN TOWARD A SEWER OPENING.
A wet, exhausted Stuart climbs up over the curb from the storm drains below. He hangs his head.

The CAMERA LOWERS and TILTS UP TO REVEAL the Littles' Brownstone. Warm lights glow from the window.

He turns absently, glancing across the street. He looks up and catches his breath.

He can't believe his great luck. He runs across the street.

> STUART (cont'd)
> I made it! I can't believe it! I'm home! Mom, Dad, I'm coming!

INT. LITTLE HOUSE – DOORWAY
The MAIL SLOT OPENS and Stuart tumbles through on to the floor. Then:

> STUART
> Mom. Dad. George. It's me, Stuart. I'm back.

INT. KITCHEN
Snowbell HEARS Stuart calling. SURPRISED, he perks up. His eyes narrow, dangerously.

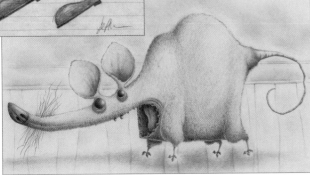

Early sketches by Sean Mullen imagined a much more cartoonlike version of Stuart than was intended for the movie.

> STUART
> Mom . . . Dad . . . George.

Snowbell heads into the living room.

INT. LIVING ROOM
Snowbell enters and sees Stuart.

> STUART
> Where is everybody?

> SNOWBELL
> There's nobody else here. It's just you. And me, kid.

> STUART
> Where'd they go?

> SNOWBELL
> Movies, I think.

> STUART
> Movies?

> SNOWBELL
> Oh, yeah. Ever since you left it's just movies, parties, roller skating, amusement parks. They're having the time of their lives.

> STUART
> They are?

> SNOWBELL
> Oh sure. Stuart, I hate to have to tell you this, but they're celebrating.

> STUART
> Celebrating what?

> SNOWBELL
> Can't you guess?

> STUART
> No.

> SNOWBELL
> They were just so happy to get rid of you.

> STUART
> That's a lie. I don't believe that.

> SNOWBELL
> Oh boy. I wish I could spare you this. This is going to break your little heart. Look up there.

> STUART (looks)
> At what?

STUART'S CAR

The first appearance of the red roadster marks an emotional high point in the movie. Stuart is overwhelmed when he sees the car. "It's the first time I've fit in since I got here," he tells George. The next time the car appears, later in the movie, George gives Stuart the roadster as a parting gift, marking a second major emotional scene.

With so much focused on this car, the filmmakers went to extraordinary lengths to create a worthy vehicle. Designed by John Bevelheimer at Imageworks, the car started out as a '50s or a '60s vehicle that was part Buick, part Cadillac. Rob Minkoff asked the artists to add an element that was mouselike and unique to Stuart but not so obvious that it dominated the car. Thus, the front grill is fashioned in the shape of a mouse's front teeth. At first, the car was yellow but eventually it evolved into a brilliant red; many variations of the color were tested.

In all, nine cars were built, each with a different purpose. The more detailed cars, with running lights and working doors, were used for close-up shots. The stunt cars were made with less detail but featured such modifications as rear-wheel drive and double-thickness fiberglass for more durability and balance on the bumpy roads. A fully waterproof car with functioning lights was created for the underwater shots and a larger-scale model was used for interiors. "The cars operated really well," says Phil Notaro of Thunderstone, the model shop that built the car bodies and interiors. (The chassis were built by Eric Allard at All-FXS.) "All aspects worked, even when John Dykstra wanted the stunt car to sink slowly in the water with all the lights on."

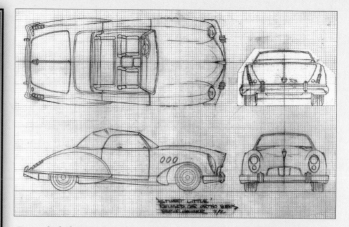

Detailed drawings of Stuart's car by John Bevelheimer.

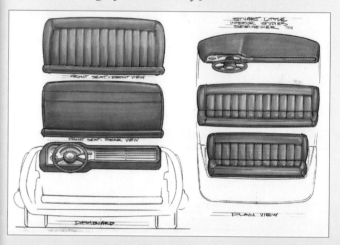

SNOWBELL
See for yourself.

STUART'S P. O. V.
The family portrait with Stuart's FACE CUT OUT.

SNOWBELL AND STUART

SNOWBELL *(cont'd)*
They did that right after you left. Mrs. Little said "who wants to look at that face anymore?"

STUART *(starting to cry)*
She did?

SNOWBELL
Yeah.

STUART
And George?

SNOWBELL
She gave it to him and he tore it up.

STUART
He did?

SNOWBELL
Yeah. I'd give you the pieces but Mr. Little set them on fire.

Stuart is CRYING.

SNOWBELL *(cont'd)*
I tried to warn you, Stuart. I told you it wasn't going to work out.

STUART
I should've known. It was too good to be true.

SNOWBELL
What are you going to do now?

STUART
I don't know. I guess I'll —

SNOWBELL
— leave immediately, good idea. I'll tell the family you dropped by. Although it'll probably just make them sick.

STUART
'Bye, Snowbell.

Left: Filmmakers shooting the back window of the roadster as it pulls away from the Little house.

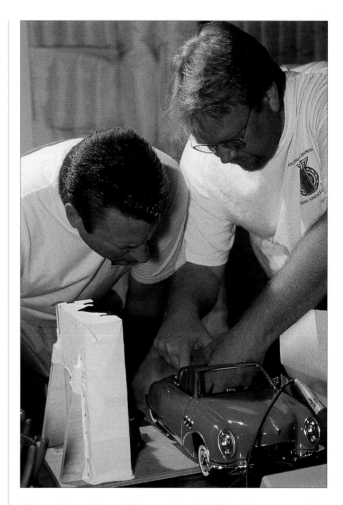

Henry Darnell, model supervisor for Thunderstone, and Curt Engelmann, lead on car, installing batteries in the roadster during a break in filming.

SNOWBELL
Good-bye, buddy. This is killing me.

EXT. CENTRAL PARK – LATE NIGHT
George works feverishly stapling "MISSING!" posters, taping one to a tree. They're up and down this pathway, some at "mouse-eye" level.

MRS. LITTLE
George.

GEORGE
I'm almost done.

MR. LITTLE
Getting late. Time to go home.

Mr. and Mrs. Little lead George away. Neither says a word. A wind comes up, blowing the stack of posters into the night.

Of the nine cars built for Stuart Little, *this is the most intricate one. This interactive model has remote controls for doors that open and close, head and taillights, and a working suspension. "The car sports an extremely high level of detail," says Phil Notaro of Thunderstone.*

The family model of the roadster was large enough to carry stuffed passengers (here the Stouts and Stuart in the back-seat) and was made for driving on smooth surfaces. This model also included many details for close-up shots.

EXT. LITTLE HOUSE

MISERABLY, Stuart crosses the street. Crying, he enters the park.

FADE OUT:

FADE IN:

INT. TAXI – MOVING – NIGHT

Wearily, Mr. and Mrs. Little and George return home.

> GEORGE
> Now all we have to do is wait until somebody calls and tells us where Stuart is.

> MR. LITTLE
> Right.

> MRS. LITTLE
> Um hmm.

Mr. and Mrs. Little exchange a look.

CUT TO:

George sits stoically in the living room, waiting for the phone to ring, as Mr. and Mrs. Little enter carrying the tea tray.

> MRS. LITTLE
> If we don't find Stuart, it's going to break his heart.

EXT. N.Y. STREET – WINDOWSILL – NIGHT

> MONTY
> Hey, Snow, one of the guys spotted Stuart in Central Park. Smokey sent me to get you.

> SNOWBELL
> Gee, Monty, I'm in for the night. It's late. Besides, Stuart's gone. Can't we just give the kid a break?

> MONTY
> Of course we can give him a break. First we'll break his little arms, then we'll break his little legs, then we'll break his little teeth. But first we gotta find him. Come on.

EXT. CENTRAL PARK – NIGHT

A pack of cats, including Snowbell and Monty run through the park.

> SMOKEY
> I think we're getting closer. I can smell him.

> LUCKY
> Sorry, Smokey, that was me.

> SMOKEY
> Around this way.

> SNOWBELL (*huffing*)
> Take it easy, fellas. The only exercise I get is rolling over.

They go on a little farther and Snowbell stops.

> SMOKEY
> Just past here. We'll spread out.

> LUCKY
> You zig, I'll zag.

> MONTY
> Why do I have to zag. I'm always zaggin'.

> SNOWBELL (*huffing*)
> You . . . you guys go ahead. I'll just . . . I'll just collapse right here.

He does. He tries to catch his breath.

> STUART
> Hey, Snow.

He sees Stuart up in a tree.

> SNOWBELL
> Uh oh. Stuart, is that you?! What are you doing up there?

> STUART
> Oh, I'm, um, settling in.

Snowbell starts to climb the tree.

> *"I read the book years ago to my kids and then reread it again for this project. I think we've got a much nicer Stuart than in the original E. B. White story. Ours is a really good guy with a good soul, a good heart, and not a devious bone in his body. He's a great role model for kids, very enthusiastic and considerate. He's the kind of guy you want your daughter to marry."*
>
> —ALAN SILVESTRI
> COMPOSER OF ORIGINAL SCORE

EXT. NEST IN TREE – NIGHT

SNOWBELL
Look, Stuart, you gotta get out of here. This is Central Park. It's dark out. There are hungry cats all over the place.

MONTY
Hey, Snow! Where are you? Come out, come out wherever you are. Snow?

Monty appears at the base of the tree.

STUART
Hey, look, it's your pal, Monty. What's he doing here?

SNOWBELL
Shhh! He'll hear you.

STUART (whispers)
Why shouldn't he hear me?

MONTY
Snowy, buddy. What are you doin' up there?

SNOWBELL
Oh no! Perfect.

MONTY
Heeyyy! You found him. Atta boy! Hey, everybody, over here! Hey, guys, Snow found him.

The cats appear and add their congratulations.

SMOKEY
Nice going, house cat. Just for that, when we carve up the mouse . . . you get the big half.

Snowbell hesitates.

STUART
Big half? Snowbell, what's he talking about? Do you know those cats?

Snowbell doesn't know what to say.

SNOWBELL
Uhhhh . . . well not really. We went to a few parties, but . . .

SMOKEY
Whatsa' matta'? What are you waiting for?

Snowbell's mind is racing — "what to do?"

MONTY
Come on, buddy. Bring him down. I'm starvin'.

SNOWBELL
Oh . . . oh . . .

STUART
Snowbell?!

SNOWBELL
Sorry, kid.

Suddenly — Snowbell grabs Stuart in his mouth. Stuart dangles over the hungry cats.

STUART

Snowbell!? Wait! No! Stop, wait! No! Put me down!

MONTY

Drop him. Bombs away.

STUART

I guess you do know them.

MONTY

Hey! Let him go. I can almost taste him. What are you waiting for?

Suddenly, Snowbell turns and rushes up the tree.

MONTY *(cont'd)*

Hey, where ya' goin'?

LUCKY

He's hogging the mouse. He ain't sharing.

SMOKEY

Get him!

LUCKY

Get up there! Let's go!

The cats scamper up the tree after the retreating Snowbell.

STUART

Snowbell, watch it. Watch it. Where're we going?

RED

Hey, hold that branch for me.

Snow finds a high branch and spits Stuart out. Stuart drops.

STUART

Snow, you saved me?

SNOWBELL

Yeah, yeah . . . Look, let's get one thing straight, I'm doing this for the Littles, all right? They love you. George loves you. They're all miserable without you . . .

STUART

But . . . Snowbell. You said—

SNOWBELL

I know what I said. I lied, okay? Welcome to Manhattan. I'm the one that hates you.

Stuart hugs Snowbell's leg.

STUART

Ah . . . Snowbell . . . you do care.

E. B. WHITE

*P*ublished in 1945, *Stuart Little* was the first children's book written by the distinguished author E. B. White. Born Elwyn Brooks White in 1899 in Mount Vernon, New York, White graduated from Cornell in 1921. After traveling and working in many different jobs, he found employment with *The New Yorker* when it was still a fledgling magazine. Over the years, he contributed numerous satirical sketches, poems, and editorials to the magazine, many of which were either unsigned or carried his initials, E.B.W. He spent most of his career writing for both *The New Yorker* and *Harper's*.

In later years, he claimed that the character of Stuart Little came to him in a dream. In a form letter he routinely sent to his fans, he wrote, "Many years ago I went to bed one night in a railway sleeping car and during the night I dreamed about a tiny boy who acted rather like a mouse. That's how the story of Stuart Little got started." He began writing *Stuart Little* to amuse a six-year-old niece and, over the years, sent her chapters in the continuing story. It took White almost seventeen years to complete the book and, by that time, his niece had grown up and was reading Hemingway.

Still, *Stuart Little* was an enormous publishing success. Never out of print in more than fifty years, the book has sold more than 25 million copies. E. B. White went on to write two other children's classics, *Charlotte's Web* in 1952 and *Trumpet of the Swan* in 1970. He received the 1970 Laura Ingalls Wilder Medal for children's books, the National Medal for Literature, the Presidential Medal of Freedom, and a special Pulitzer Prize for his body of work.

E. B. White died in 1985.

SNOWBELL (*embarrassed*)

Uhhh . . . Yeah, yeah, okay, okay, that's enough.

The cats surround them on lower branches and Smokey climbs up behind them.

MONTY

Snow, what's he doing to your leg?

Snowbell looks away, embarrassed.

MONTY (*cont'd*)

I can't help but think this is wrong.

SMOKEY

What the hell's going on here?

SNOWBELL

Uhhh . . . Look, Smokey, call me fickle, but I want to call this whole thing off, okay?

ALAN SILVESTRI ON THE MUSIC

One of the special challenges in scoring a movie like this is that, like an animated film, it is created in layers. Even though I was involved very early on, still, the movie itself only comes into focus over a period of time. Every couple of weeks you get to see a little more of what the movie will be, so some versions I saw didn't have Stuart at all, some had Stuart as a gray mouse, some had a stuffed Stuart on a stick. It wasn't until fairly recently that I saw the finished Stuart and that just took my breath away. But this is the problem with scoring all-animated movies or any films that are optically oriented with heavy-duty special effects.

To score a film, I sit down with the director and we watch the movie together. We spend anywhere from a half day to three days going through the film, reel by reel, and deciding where the film is calling for music. This is called a spotting session.

From the very beginning, Rob talked about finding a kind of hybrid solution to the music that would be influenced by the '40s but be part of the '90s in terms of the point of view of the score and how it plays the dramatic aspects of the film. I tried to find a sound that would correspond to the setting of the film, which is really a mix of images.

The film combines a kind of 1940s timeless New York with elements of the 1990s. George comes into the room with a backpack. You never quite know what year the movie is taking place. This gives you a lot of freedom with the music, but also it gives you a lot of rope to hang yourself. I really was looking for a sound that would correspond to the overall image of the film and fit the range of possibilities presented in the film. So we have a big-band influence surrounded by the orchestra. I think this works with the look of the movie and is similar to the kinds of solutions found in other parts of the movie—like the production design and the costumes, for example.

Another challenge is that the style of the movie has an animation consciousness that alternates with straight dramatic scenes. You go from the chase in the kitchen scene, which is almost an out-and-out cartoon, but then the film does a 180 and you are in a dramatic scene and have to score for a live-action moment. It's like a live-action cartoon. The music has to allow for the very interesting fabric that makes this movie so effective.

SMOKEY
Too late.

SNOWBELL
Come on, Smokey. Can't we talk it over? You know, Stuart's not so bad once you get to know him. And he's got his own car.

SMOKEY
Careful, house cat, you're asking for it.

MONTY
Snow, what are you doing? Come on, he's just a mouse.

SNOWBELL
He's not just a mouse. He's family.

SMOKEY
Oh, yeah, I can see the resemblance.

The cats laugh.

STUART
Is that what you think? That you have to look alike to be family?

The cats are all drawn to attention.

STUART
You don't have to look alike, you don't even have to like each other. Look at Snowbell. He hates me and still, he's trying to save me. Sure you'll probably scratch him up pretty bad, you'll tear him to shreads. You may even kill him, but Snowbell will not run away . . . and that's what family's all about. Right, Snow?

SNOWBELL
Maybe family's too strong of a word.

SMOKEY
Scratch 'em both.

SNOWBELL
Both?!

Stuart quickly unfastens Snowbell's collar and loops the collar over a nearby branch and—

STUART (suddenly, to the cats)
Hey! It's me you want. Come and get me.

He grabs the loop and jumps. The collar slides down a long branch.

BOONE NARR ON THE CATS

A cat is probably the most difficult of all animals to train. Then you add a second or a third cat and by leaps and bounds it just gets harder and harder. Here there were eight cat characters, which meant there were eight trainers we had to hide out of the scene, and our biggest undertaking was to then get all the cats to work together, in character, as a unit.

We picked four cats for each character so we had backups and stand-ins for each one of them. We had our stunt cats and our close-up cats. During the course of the day of filming, we were constantly interchanging cats.

Casting the cats went on for months. We went to all the cat shows around California and picked cats. We tried them out to see if they fit their characters in the movie. They also had to match the voices of the actors who were doing the voices. It took endless amounts of preparation.

We started with the storyboards, as our bible, to train the cats to do what we needed them to do. But these kinds of movies are like sponges. They just grow and grow; the scenes get bigger and bigger and more complicated. We arrived on the set really early each day to find our spots and work out the lighting and such. Truthfully, you can really do only so much training and the rest is pure luck. There's a lot of luck involved in getting the animals to stop looking at their trainers and to really interact with the other characters in the movie.

Animal trainer Boone Narr and the Second Unit Assistant Director Frederic Roth discussing a scene in which the cats are having a conversation in the Little house.

The second unit film crew shooting Snowbell crossing the street at the end of the movie.

The most difficult cat scenes to shoot were those with the group of cats. Here, trainers and cats work together filming a scene from the end of the movie. Mark Harden watches over Monty, Shawn Weber works with Lucky, and Debbie Jacobsohn oversees Smokey.

STUART (cont'd)
Yee haa!

SMOKEY
Get him!

He jets past the cats as they swing wildly at him.

RED (ad lib)
Get him! Get him! He's gettin' away.

The branch ends in the darkness — Stuart flies into space and grabs a tree tip — Where he holds on for dear life as the collar disappears in the darkness. It is a long time before we hear it hit . . . water.

Stuart YELLS as he falls and then grabs the branch.

Stuart clings on. His little weight bends the tip of the branch down toward lower branches — which to his horror starts to become crowded with the gang cats.

RED
Where is he? Did he fall in the water?

LUCKY
I saw something hit.

Monty climbs out onto the branch.

MONTY
Man, did you see that? Gone. He just disappeared. (looking up) Whoa. Huh? There he is.

LUCKY
Huh?

MONTY
Up there.

The cats see Stuart hanging.

MONTY
He's too far. Can't reach him.

They look up expectantly but he is well out of reach.

STUART
In that case, you can all go home. Prowl safely.

Suddenly his branch bends lower — something's wrong. Stuart looks up to see Smokey adding his weight to the little branch. Now he is just out of reach.

SMOKEY
Here you go, boys . . . dinner's served.

MONTY
All right, Smokey! Way to go!

STUART
Oh dear.

LUCKY
Look, it's mouse on a stick. I love mouse on a stick.

MONTY
A little further! Keep him coming! Keep him coming! Right, I can almost reach him. Keep it coming! I got him, he's mine.

Stuart closes his eyes and readies for the worst. The branch below suddenly cracks under added weight. Everyone holds on for dear life.

ALL THE CATS (ad lib)
Whoa! Uh, hey! Careful!

MONTY
The branch is gonna . . . !

The branch cracks again.

Snowbell is pressing down the cat-loaded branch — it splinters under his paw.

SNOWBELL
Well, what do we got here?

MONTY
Snow, don't come out here. The branch is breakin'!

SNOWBELL
Stuart! Are you all right?

STUART
Yeah. Yeah, I'm okay.

SNOWBELL
Just hang on. I'll take it from here.

MONTY
Huh? Take what? (*realizes Snowbell's pushing the branch*) Come on, Snow, you wouldn't do this to me . . . not your old buddy.

SNOWBELL
Don't worry, buddy. I'm sure you'll land on your feet.

MONTY
Hey, Snow, what're you doin'? Nooo, don't! Wait! Stop! Wait! I gotta ask you somethin'!

Crack — The branch snaps and six cats fall and fall — right into the lake.

CATS (*falling*)
Aaaah!

(*coughing*)

They paddle for shore and limp off into the night.

Monty climbs out of the pond.

CATS (*ad lib*)
Whew! Cold, cold, very cold.

MONTY
How could he do this to me? After all we meant to each other. I mean, I loved that guy. Hey, you guys. Wait up for me!

Meanwhile high up in the tree.

SNOWBELL
Pack up the pineapple, Stuart. This luau's over.

STUART
Thanks, Snowbell. You were great.

SNOWBELL
Well, it must have been quite a show from up there.

STUART
Snowbell.

SNOWBELL
Those cats think they're so tough.

STUART
Snowbell.

SNOWBELL
I guess I showed them. Not bad for a house cat.

He turns and comes whisker to whisker with Smokey.

SMOKEY
Not bad for a dead house cat. Say good night, Tinkerbell.

A frightened Snowbell is backed up along the branch by Smokey.

STUART (O.S.)
Hey, Smokey.

Stuart has gotten to an adjoining fork of the tree and pulled back a long sapling — like a slender bent whip.

STUART (*cont'd*)
His name is Snowbell.

He lets the sapling go — Smokey looks just in time to catch a face full of sapling.

THE CATS IN CENTRAL PARK

*I*n the third act, Stuart returns from the Stouts' castle in Brooklyn, crossing the bridge and then passing through Central Park where the cats are waiting to ambush him. Central Park was actually several different sets. The paths and benches were on one stage. The gully was on another stage. Stuart racing backward down the hill was on yet another stage, as was the scene where the roadster splashes into the storm drain.

And then there were the cats.

In most cases, the action would be storyboarded for review with Rob Minkoff. Boone Narr and his animal trainers would review the cat action several days in advance of the shoot. The cats would then be trained on the set where they would work. We were planning to add mouth movement and some face manipulation to the cats as a special effect, but we wanted to capture as much timing, expression, and body language as possible in the live-action photography. We would always try to photograph the action as it was in the storyboards, but there were times when a cat, or cats, simply didn't want to do what we had planned. We learned to be flexible and, in fact, some of the cat improvisation was better than what we had originally scripted.

—JOHN DYKSTRA, SENIOR VISUAL EFFECTS SUPERVISOR AND SECOND-UNIT DIRECTOR

SMOKEY
AAAAAAHHHHH!

Smokey gets blasted out of the tree and crashes into the pond.

He swims away, defeated.

Stuart and Snowbell gazing down at Smokey in the water.

STUART
Little hi little lo.

SNOWBELL
Little hey little ho.

SNOWBELL *(cont'd)*
Let's go home.

CUT TO:
Snowball and Stuart hop down from the last bit of tree trunk and onto the ground.

CUT TO:
EXT. LITTLE HOUSE – NIGHT
Snowbell sings the baseline to "Happy Trails" and Stuart sings the words as they round the corner toward the Little house, Stuart riding on Snowbell's back.

STUART
Here we are, Snow. Home at last.

SNOWBELL
Can I stop now?

Snowbell leaps up onto the window ledge. Stuart climbs off.

Snowbell looks at Stuart. Sighs.

STUART
Thanks for the ride!.

Stuart hugs Snowbell tight. After a long BEAT . . .

SNOWBELL
Don't mention it . . . ever!

INT. LITTLE HOME – LIVING ROOM- NIGHT
A fire glows in the fireplace. George is fast asleep in a chair, the phone still in his lap.

Mr. and Mrs. Little enter, and gently take the phone from George. Mr. Little lifts George into his arms and begins carrying him from the living room to the hallway. A cuckoo clock sounds and George's eyes flutter open . . . His mouth opens.

Artist Thor Freudenthal's storyboard drawing of the moment when Stuart hugs Snowbell's leg for saving him from the other cats, a scene that made it to the final film. Rob Minkoff described Snowbell's expression here as "a Jack Benny." Amazingly enough, during filming, the cat playing Snowbell performed a kind of double take that was exactly what the director wanted.

GEORGE
Stuart!

Mr. and Mrs. Little turn sharply and look over. They scream "Stuart!" but we can't hear them either. They put George down and all three rush to the window.

STUART
Mom! Dad! George!

Mrs. Little, Mr. Little, and George all start talking at the same time. Their faces are right up to the glass with Stuart's. Mrs. Little starts to cry.

Stuart speaks at the glass.

STUART *(cont'd)*
I missed you all so much. I thought I'd never see you again!

The Littles are so excited. They just keep on talking.

Mr. Little realizes how silly they look and he suddenly throws open the window.

GEORGE
Stuart, I knew you'd come back!

MR. LITTLE
Are you okay?

MRS. LITTLE
I can't believe it.

MR. LITTLE
I don't understand. How did you manage it?

A long BEAT as Stuart considers . . .

STUART
Every Little in the world can find the Little
house . . . And Snowbell . . .

Stuart glances at Snowbell.

STUART (cont'd)
. . . I couldn't have done it without him.

Mr. Little scoops up Snowbell, strokes him. Mrs. Little
scoops up Stuart. Everybody stands, overwhelmed, in
the living room. Stuart gets choked up.

MR. LITTLE
What's the matter?

STUART
I was just thinking . . .

MRS. LITTLE
What, dear?

STUART
. . . that this is how people look . . .

GEORGE
. . . at the end of a fairy tale?

*As he peered into the great land that
stretched before him, the way seemed long.
But the sky was bright, and he somehow
felt he was headed in the right direction.*
—E. B. WHITE, *STUART LITTLE*, 1945

Stuart gazes at his mother, father, brother, and Snowbell.

STUART
Yeah. Exactly.

They turn to leave, then George turns back, leaps into
the window seat and closes the shade.

We pull back from the modest brownstone, their happy
shadows falling on the shade . . .

Stuart may be right. This may be the most beautiful
house in the whole world.

FADE OUT
EXT. LITTLE HOUSE – NIGHT
The camera pulls away from the window and ascends
the front of the Littles' house and up into the star-filled
night sky.

THE END

CREDITS

---

*One morning when the wind was from
the west, Stuart . . . set out for a walk,
full of the joy of life and the fear of dogs.*

—E. B. WHITE, *STUART LITTLE*, 1945

THE FILMMAKERS

ROB MINKOFF (Director)

Director Rob Minkoff codirected the groundbreaking blockbuster animated film *The Lion King*. A graduate of Cal Arts' character animation program, Minkoff began his relationship with Walt Disney as an animator, contributing to character design and story development on such animated features as *The Little Mermaid* and *Beauty and the Beast*.

He made his directorial debut on the Roger Rabbit shorts *Tummy Trouble* and *Roller Coaster Rabbit*. He also acted as coproducer of the third installment, *Trail Mix-Up*.

Minkoff expanded into the live-action world directing *Mickey's Audition*, a short film for the MGM Studio Theme Park in Orlando, Florida. *Mickey's Audition* combined live action and animation with cameos from such celebrities as Mel Brooks and Angela Lansbury.

Born in Palo Alto, California, Minkoff now makes his home in Los Angeles.

DOUGLAS WICK (Producer)

Including *Stuart Little*, Douglas Wick and his Columbia Pictures–based Red Wagon Productions have produced four major motion pictures this year. *Girl, Interrupted*, a Columbia holiday release, was directed by the critically acclaimed director James Mangold. The film stars two of the most touted young actresses working today, Academy Award® nominee Winona Ryder and two-time Golden Globe winner Angelina Jolie, as well as costarring Academy Award® winners Vanessa Redgrave and Whoopi Goldberg. It is based on the best-selling book of the same name.

Wick's next release will be the epic *Gladiator*, which was directed by Academy Award® nominee Ridley Scott and stars Russell Crowe and Joaquin Phoenix. Set in second-century Rome, this lavish production constructed an almost full-scale replica of the Coliseum on the island of Malta.

The final Wick production to be released in 2000 is the Paul Verhoeven thriller *The Hollow Man*, which stars Academy Award® nominee Elisabeth Shue and Kevin Bacon. This shocking suspense thriller is about a scientist who develops a formula for invisibility and goes into a sinister and terrifying tailspin when he successfully tests the drug on himself.

Next up for the versatile Wick will be Steven Spielberg's highly anticipated *Memoirs of a Geisha*; the book of this work has been on the *New York Times* hardcover and paperback best-seller lists for more than 102 weeks.

Wick's Red Wagon Productions is a story-based company whose collaboration with a remarkable ensemble of writers has developed screenplays that have attracted some of the most accomplished filmmakers in the world.

Wick has produced two movies by Academy Award®–winning director Mike Nichols. The most recent was *Wolf*, starring Jack Nicholson and Michelle Pfeiffer. Wick's first producing effort, which Nichols also directed, was *Working Girl*, starring Harrison Ford, Melanie Griffith, and Sigourney Weaver. The film garnered six Academy Award® nominations, including Best Picture and Best Song (which Carly Simon won for her single "Let the River Run"). It also won five Golden Globes, including Best Picture for Wick.

After graduating *cum laude* from Yale University, Wick began his career as a coffee boy for filmmaker Alan Pakula, for whom he was associate producer on *Starting Over*. Wick has also produced two other movies for Columbia, including *Hush*, starring Gwyneth Paltrow and Jessica Lange, and *The Craft*, starring Neve Campbell.

JASON CLARK (Executive Producer)

Jason Clark produced the TriStar Pictures release of Steven Gyllenhall's *Homegrown*, starring Billy Bob Thornton, and the upcoming *Hacks*, a Lion's Gate comedy about television writers in Hollywood, starring Stephen Rea and Illeana Douglas, with Tom Arnold, Ryan O'Neal, Lisa Kudrow, and John Ritter. Clark also executive produced *Happy, Texas,* starring William H. Macy, Jeremy Northam, and Steve Zahn.

Other film producing credits include Jean Claude Van Damme's *Maximum Risk, Sudden Death,* and *The Quest.*

Clark was born in New York City and began his career in the entertainment industry as a production assistant for Walter Hill and Larry Gordon on the film *Streets of Fire.*

A graduate of UCLA in economics, Clark served as vice president for Smart Egg Pictures as well as in several other production and development positions. He is also a member of the Director's Guild of America.

GREG BROOKER (Screenwriter)

Stuart Little is Greg Brooker's first produced screenplay. He has sold several screenplays, including *Meet Your Dream Date* to Artisan, *The Tooth Fairy* to Disney, *Universal Baseball* to Paramount, *My Summer, My Honeymoon,* to Avenue, *They Don't Dance Much* to Propaganda, *Max Lakeman and the Beautiful Stranger* to Columbia, and *Living Like Kings* to Cinecorp. He also wrote the screenplays *Fall and Rise of Glen* and *Spring '61.*

M. NIGHT SHYAMALAN (Screenwriter)

M. Night Shyamalan most recently earned acclaim as a director with the phenomenal success of the summer blockbuster *The Sixth Sense.* Shyamalan also wrote the screenplay for the film, which starred Bruce Willis, Toni Collette, and Haley Joel Osment.

Shyamalan began making films at the age of ten in his hometown of Philadelphia. At sixteen, he had completed his forty-fifth short film. At age seventeen, he stood before his parents, both doctors, surrounded by pictures of the other twelve doctors in the family, and informed them that although he graduated *cum laude* and received academic scholarships to several prestigious medical programs, he had instead decided to attend New York University Tisch School of the Arts to study filmmaking.

In the fall of 1992, he found himself on a plane to India with the funding to make his first low-budget feature film, based on a screenplay he had written during his final year at NYU. *Praying with Anger* is the very personal story of an exchange student from the United States who goes back to India and finds himself a stranger in his own homeland. Shyamalan served as writer, director, producer, and star of the film, which garnered praise from the Toronto Film Festival, was selected to be screened by the New York Foundation of the Arts' prestigious First Look Series, and in July 1993 was named Debut Film of the Year by the American Film Institute in Los Angeles.

One year later, he took his spiritual storytelling to the next level when he sold his original screenplay *Labor of Love* to Twentieth Century-Fox. In 1997 his second feature film, *Wide Awake,* which starred Joseph Cross, Rosie O'Donnell, Denis Leary, Dana Delaney, and Robert Loggia, was released theatrically. That film was shot entirely in and around the Philadelphia area and tells the story of the close relationship between a boy in Catholic school and his grandfather.

GUILLERMO NAVARRO (Director of Photography)

Director of photography Guillermo Navarro was born and raised in Mexico City, where he entered into the world of cinema. Before relocating to the United States in 1994, he lent his talents to such films shot on location in Mexico as Guillermo Del Toro's *Cronos,* which garnered the Grand Prize, International Critics Week at the 1993 Cannes Film Festival; Nicholas Echevarria's *Cabeza de Vaca,* nominated for a Best Cinematography Award at the Mexican Academy Awards; *Mambo,* directed by Paul Leduc; Alberto Cortes's *Amor a la Vuelta de la Esquina*; and the Dutch production of Joss de Paww's *Vinaya.*

Navarro has shot an eclectic group of features, including the critically acclaimed *Jackie Brown* with director Quentin Tarantino and *Four Rooms, Desperado,* and *From Dusk Till Dawn* for director Robert Rodriguez. Other film credits include *Spawn* and *The Long Kiss Goodnight.*

For television, Navarro's credits include "Mayas," a one-hour National Geographic Society special for which he was nominated for a 1994 Emmy for Best Cinematography, *The Cisco Kid* for TNT, and Michael Lindsay's *The Hit List* for KCET.

BILL BRZESKI (Production Designer)

Production designer Bill Brzeski lent his design talents to the Oscar®-winning *As Good As It Gets* as well as to *Matilda*. He also served as the art director on *I'll Do Anything*.

With credits on over eight hundred episodes of television, Brzeski is highly regarded for his extensive accomplishments in the television field.

Brzeski received his undergraduate degree from Miami University in Ohio and his Master of Fine Arts in Design from New York University's Tisch School of the Arts. Originally interested in designing for the ballet and opera, he began his career in theater.

Brzeski was born in Burbank, California, and was raised in Boston, Massachusetts.

JOSEPH PORRO (Costume Designer)

Costume designer Joseph Porro has designed such blockbusters as *Godzilla* and *Independence Day* (a Saturn Award nominee). Other film credits include *Homegrown, The Quest, Mighty Morphin Power Rangers, Stargate, Tombstone, Super Mario Brothers, Universal Soldier, Meet the Applegates,* and *Near Dark*.

Born in Boston, Porro attended UCLA, majoring in costuming for film and television, and the Parsons School of Design, majoring in fashion design. He began his career training as an assistant designer to such fashion greats as Halston and Geoffrey Beene.

TOM FINAN (Editor)

Editor Tom Finan cut the record-breaking animated hit feature *The Lion King* (for which he shared credit) as well as *Hercules* and the upcoming, highly anticipated animated feature *Kingdom of the Sun*.

Other film credits include *Pet Sematary II, It Had to Be You, The Wizard, Problem Child* (as second editor), *Platoon, Salvador,* and *What's Love Got to Do With It* (for additional editing).

A native Angeleno, Finan has worked on such television series as *Tales from the Crypt,* among others, and the telefilms *Where Have They Taken Our Children: The Chowchilla Kidnapping Story,* TNT's *Grand Isle, Writer's Block, Desperado,* and *Combat High*.

JOHN DYKSTRA (Senior Visual Effects Supervisor)

Visual effects wizard John Dykstra won a Visual Effects Academy Award® for his work on *Star Wars* as well as an Academy Technical Achievement Award for Industrial Light and Magic. Dykstra was instrumental in the founding of the now world-renowned Industrial Light and Magic with Gary Kurtz and George Lucas. Dykstra arranged the creative team to design and build the *Star Wars* miniatures and camera systems.

Dykstra came to the entertainment industry with a background in industrial design and still photography. In his early days, he worked building models and doing effects photography, as well as designing, building, and operating a computer-controlled camera system for the National Science Foundation at the University of California at Berkeley. This sophisticated camera would later be acknowledged as the foundation of motion-control technology.

Dykstra went on to produce and serve as visual effects supervisor on *Battlestar Galactica,* working with his key creative team from *Star Wars* in their newly formed company, Apogee. Using Apple's first personal computers as the basis for its motion-imaging systems, Apogee garnered an Emmy for its *Battlestar Galactica* work.

While at Apogee, Dykstra's effects team captured an Academy Award® nomination for *Star Trek: The Movie,* and Dykstra continued contributing to visual effects for many feature films, entertainment theme parks, and video games. He also directed commercials. Under Dykstra's guidance, Apogee developed benchmark motion-control and blue-screen technologies.

Most recently, Dykstra was visual effects supervisor on *Batman Forever* and *Batman & Robin*. He joined Imageworks in March 1998 to supervise visual effects and direct second unit for *Stuart Little*.

HENRY F. ANDERSON III (Animation Supervisor)

A graduate of California Institute of the Arts' character animation program, Henry F. Anderson III has worked as a director of digital character animation for the past ten years. His specialty is creating convincing, believable digital actors.

He has directed projects at Pacific Data Images (PDI), Rhythm&Hues, Pixar, Blue Sky, Digital Domain, and now Sony Pictures Imageworks. These have included both all-animated projects as well as live-action/animation combinations. He has been responsible for creating the performances of several digitally animated "spokes characters" for national and international campaigns, including the Polar Bears for Coca-Cola.

In addition to several Clio Awards, Henry won a Prime Time Emmy for *The Last Halloween*, a CBS/Hanna-Barbera special that was the first television production to feature digital lead characters within a live-action show. The creation of Romtu, Gleep, Scoota, and Bing, the four Martians who visit Earth on Halloween night in search of candy, was a milestone in animation.

Outside of his directing assignments, Henry has taught character design at Cal Arts and has given talks and presentations about digital character animation in North and South America, in Europe, and in Asia.

Before attending Cal Arts, Henry studied biology at University of California San Diego where he worked with lots and lots of mice.

JEROME CHEN (Visual Effects Supervisor)

One of the motion picture industry's most innovative visual effects supervisors, Jerome Chen combines an artistic approach with technical savvy. He joined Imageworks shortly after its inception in 1992 and worked his way up through the production ranks as a digital artist, going on to become a senior animator, computer graphics supervisor, and now visual effects supervisor. His credits include *Godzilla, Contact, James and the Giant Peach, Phenomenon, The Ghost and the Darkness,* and *In the Line of Fire.*

An acknowledged expert in the technique of integrating live action with digital elements, Chen won the 1998 International Monitor Award for his work on the Robert Zemeckis film *Contact,* and also received Monitor nominations for *Godzilla* and *James and the Giant Peach.* Chen was also honored with a 1998 ANNIE Award nomination for his effects animation work on *Godzilla.* In 1996 he taught a digital compositing course at SIGGRAPH computer graphics conference with Ron Brinkman. He has also been a guest speaker at the UCLA computer animation graduate program. Prior to joining Imageworks, Jerome worked as a 3-D and paintbox artist at various post-production houses on both the east and west coasts. Jerome studied visual arts and English literature at the University of Maryland at College Park.

ERIC ALLARD (Special Effects Supervisor)

Special effects supervisor Eric Allard has worked on such films as *Alien Resurrection, Virus, Mission: Impossible, Demolition Man, Teenage Mutant Ninja Turtles III, FX2,* and *Trilogy of Terror II.*

Allard worked as a special-effects technician on *One from the Heart, Brainstorm,* and *Let's Go,* which featured robot PAL, one of the highlights of Japan's '85 expo. PAL captured the attention of director John Badham, who hired Allard as robotics effects supervisor for *Short Circuit* and as associate producer on *Short Circuit 2.* He created robot "Number Five," the main character. He also was second unit director on *Class of 1999.*

For television, Allard created the prosthetic makeup for *Alien Nation, Matt Houston,* and the popular pink bunny for the Energizer commercial.

Born in Syracuse, New York, Allard was raised in Phoenix, Arizona, and Southern California, and eventually enlisted in the army. After qualifying as a Green Beret Engineer Specialist, he was trained for Airborne Ranger, Advanced Demolitions, Jungle Expert, and Sniper School and graduated with honors.

He received an honorable discharge from the army and landed a job at

Universal Studios as a propmaker in the construction department. His first effects job was working in the robotic prop department on *The Black Hole,* and then on features such as *Noah's Ark, Dragonslayer, Sudden Impact,* and *Ghostbusters.*

BOONE NARR (Animal Stunt Coordinator)

Boone Narr is the owner of a multinational animal-training facility, Boone's Animals for Hollywood, Inc. Internationally known and respected in his field, Narr has filmed all over the United States and in fourteen countries around the world with his dogs, cats, and exotic animals.

Narr's training talents can be seen in DreamWorks' *Mouse Hunt* and *Paulie,* as well as *The Parent Trap, Buddy, Indiana Jones and the Last Crusade, Tarzan* (with Bo Derek), *The Accidental Tourist,* and *Batman & Robin,* among others. His training talents can also be seen in the upcoming *Mumford* and *The Green Mile.*

For television, Narr trained *Mad About You's* Murray the dog for six seasons and also supplies *7th Heaven* with their dog, Happy, and *Dharma and Greg* with their Welsh Corgie, Nunzio. Other television series include *Cybill, The Nanny, Tarzan,* and *White Fang.*

Narr has been supplying trained animals and coordinating large animal productions for Hollywood for more than twenty-six years.

ALAN SILVESTRI (Composer of Original Score)

Alan Silvestri has provided the distinctively melodic voice for some of Hollywood's most popular films, receiving Oscar® and Golden Globe nominations for the wistful melodies that accompanied *Forrest Gump* on a journey through American history. Silvestri's fanfare provided the fuel for a time-traveling DeLorean in the *Back to the Future* trilogy, which brought him two Grammy nominations. The composer's angelic chorus showed us the wonders hidden in *The Abyss,* and he's created the brassy heroism that's helped Arnold Schwarzenegger to conquer the formidable villains of *Predator* and *Eraser.*

With over sixty scores to his credit, Alan Silvestri is one of the film industry's most in-demand composers, showing his diverse talents in such soundtracks as *The Bodyguard, Romancing the Stone, Soapdish, Young Guns II, Grumpy* and *Grumpier Old Men, Father of the Bride I* and *II, Blown Away,* and *Who Framed Roger Rabbit?*

In the years 2000 and 2001, Alan is slated to compose the scores for *What Lies Beneath,* starring Harrison Ford and Michelle Pfieffer, and *Castaway,* starring Tom Hanks. Both films are directed by Robert Zemeckis.

Yet it's *Forrest Gump* that remains Alan Silvestri's most heartfelt work, a film whose remarkable poignancy and music touched the world's audiences, winning 1994's Oscar® for Best Picture. The emotion that fills its score reaches into the composer's own triumphs over personal adversity. In 1992 Alan's son, Joseph, was diagnosed with juvenile diabetes. Since this time, Alan and his wife, Sandra, have committed themselves to delivering on the promise they made to their son—a cure for diabetes.

E. B. WHITE (Author of the book *Stuart Little,* 1945)

E. B. White is a multiple award–winning writer whose editorial essays and children's books are read and treasured around the world. Born Elwyn Brooks White in 1899 in Mount Vernon, New York, White attended Cornell University and worked as a reporter and advertising copywriter until joining *The New Yorker* in 1926, where he wrote editorial essays. White spent most of his career writing for *The New Yorker's* weekly magazine and for *Harpers.*

White wrote three books for children: *Stuart Little* was the first in 1945, followed by *Charlotte's Web* in 1952, and *Trumpet of the Swan* in 1970. *Stuart Little,* illustrated by Garth Williams, remains one of his most popular and widely loved writings. White died in 1985, shortly after receiving a special Pulitzer Prize for his body of work.

SONY PICTURES IMAGEWORKS

(Special Visual Effects and "Stuart Little Designs Fabrication")

Sony Pictures Imageworks is an award-winning, state-of-the-art digital production company dedicated to the art and artistry of visual effects and computer animation. The company has lent its groundbreaking talent and technology to such films as *Big Daddy, Patch Adams, Snow Falling on Cedars, Godzilla, City of Angels, Contact, Anaconda, Michael, The Ghost and the Darkness, James and the Giant Peach,* and the Academy Award–nominated *Starship Troopers.* Imageworks is currently at work on Paul Verhoeven's *The Hollow Man*; two films for Robert Zemeckis, *Cast Away* and *What Lies Beneath*; Mike Nichols's *What Planet Are You From?*; and Imageworks president Ken Ralston's directorial debut, *Jumanji II.*

Imageworks continues to redefine the role of digital effects in feature films. From the creation of photo-real, three-dimensional, performance-based characters to celestial journeys across the universe, Imageworks artists bring filmmakers' visions to the screen. More and more, Imageworks is working with filmmakers earlier in the development cycle of feature film projects to explore the outer boundaries of possibility and invent new and novel situations and techniques.

Imageworks has grown exponentially during the past five years in terms of physical size, artistic talent, and digital infrastructure. With the arrival of Ken Ralston in late 1995 as its president and Tim Sarnoff in 1997 as its executive vice president and general manager, the company now has more than 350 artists, engineers, technicians, and support staff housed in a 120,000-square-foot facility designed by and for the next generation of digital production.

Part of this expansion at Imageworks included the creation of the Digital Character Group, supervised by Barry Weiss (*Cats Don't Dance, Pagemaster*), senior vice president of animation production, and Eric Armstrong (*Jurassic Park, Casper),* animation director. The group now numbers thirty, and their work on such films as *Anaconda, James and the Giant Peach, Contact,* and *Starship Troopers* has been recognized around the world with awards. These include the World Animation Celebrations Award for Best Character/Creature Animation for *Anaconda* and inclusion in the annual juried SIGGRAPH Computer Animation Film Festival.

Sony Pictures Imageworks is part of Sony Pictures Entertainment's Digital Studios Division. The division comprises all of the studio's technology-driven businesses including Imageworks, The High Definition Center, The DVD Center, Digital Post Production Facilities, Advanced Digital Systems Group, Advanced Entertainment Systems, Worldwide Satellite Operations, and Worldwide Product Fulfillment.

DEBBIE DENISE (Vice President, Sony Pictures Imageworks)

Debbie Denise was named Vice President of Sony Pictures Imageworks in 1995. After receiving her B.F.A. in Broadcasting from the University of Cincinnati, Ms. Denise worked as a director of live shows for the Ohio-based theme park Kings Island. Relocating to Los Angeles, she became a production manager with Paramount Sound Systems. She then moved to a position with ABC Entertainment, where she was an on-air writer-producer and was responsible for the highly successful on-air promotion for the hit series *Dynasty* in the 1980s.

Ms. Denise relocated to San Francisco in the late '80s, where she worked as a freelance video producer for interactive computer systems. She also produced audio-visual presentations for the Norwegian and Cunard cruise lines.

In 1991 Ms. Denise began work at Industrial Light and Magic, where her first position was that of visual effects coordinator. She quickly was promoted to Visual Effects Producer while at ILM, where she produced the effects for *Death Becomes Her, Forrest Gump, Tales from the Crypt, The American President,* and *Sabrina.* In April 1995, she was named Interim Head of Production for ILM, where she remained until joining Imageworks in the fall of 1995.

In addition to her role as SPI's Vice President, she has served as senior visual effects producer on Robert Zemeckis's *Contact* and *Snow Falling on Cedars,* and executive producer of visual effects on *Stuart Little, Cast Away, What Lies Beneath,* and the upcoming *Jumanji II.*

MICHELLE MURDOCCA (Senior Visual Effects Producer)

Prior to joining Sony Pictures Imageworks, Ms. Murdocca was executive producer of digital imaging at VIFX, working on such films as *The Relic, Going West,* and *Volcano.*

Also among her other credits are manager of Digital Production at Boss Film Studios, where she worked on such films as *Multiplicity, Species,* and *Outbreak.* Prior to that she was a production resources coordinator for Walt Disney Pictures.

Michelle pursued an M.A. from Cal State Northridge in Counseling Psychology with an emphasis in business and industry and a B.A. in Psychology from Roger Williams University in Bristol, Rhode Island.

JAY K. REDD (CG Supervisor Sony Pictures Imageworks)

Presently functioning as CG Supervisor on Columbia Picture's *Stuart Little,* Jay has supervised the technical and aesthetic research and development for the film's extensive hair, fur, and lighting requirements. As an amateur astronomer, he animated and supervised *Contact's* opening shot, a 4,710-frame journey from earth to the end of the universe, which has received many international awards.

Before joining Imageworks, Jay spent four years at Rhythm & Hues Studios, where he worked on numerous features, including the Academy Award–winning *Babe* and the award-winning *Seafari,* in addition to commercials and theme-park rides. Jay studied at the University of Utah with an emphasis in film, music, and Japanese.

JIM BERNEY (CG Supervisor Sony Pictures Imageworks)

Jim Berney is a staff member of the Sony Pictures Imageworks Digital Production team and Senior Computer Graphics Supervisor, providing technical direction for production modeling, texturing, and lighting pipelines. Mr. Berney joined Imageworks in 1996 from MetroLight, where he was a Research Technical Director and part of the Software Development team, authoring flocking software for *Batman Forever* and procedural natural phenomenon lighting software for *Undersiege 2* and *Mortal Combat.*

Mr. Berney received his masters degree in Computer Science from California Polytechnic, San Luis Obispo, specializing in the research and development of a new global illumination paradigm. He holds two undergraduate degrees in Computer Science and Economics from the University of California, Irvine, focusing in AI research for NASA under the guidance of Pat Langely. Jim also studied computer architectures at the Royal Institute of Technology, Stockholm, Sweden. After graduation, Jim worked for three years for DARPA as an ADA programmer for a large software engineering consortium.

At Imageworks, Jim served as CG Supervisor on the feature film *Stuart Little* and was involved in the beginning stages of developing the costuming technology that enabled the design, building, and simulation of thirteen costumes for three CG characters. Jim also supervised the development of the versioning and publishing system and co-supervised the development of the lighting pipeline that facilitated the seamless integration of the Stuart Little character into live-action scenes. Prior to *Stuart Little,* Jim served as CG Supervisor on the feature films *Godzilla* and lighting lead on *Contact, Starship Troopers,* and *Anaconda,* where he developed rendering tools and the pipeline for photorealistic lighting techniques. Jim's research interests are in the area of global illumination, artificial intelligence, neural networks, and version and publishing.

SCOTT STOKDYK (CG Supervisor Sony Pictures Imageworks)

As one of the CG Supervisors on *Stuart Little,* Scott focused on the character and animation setup pipeline while also supervising multicharacter shots in many different sequences. In addition, he helped develop and lead the effects work and create various composite setups that were used on *Stuart* elements.

While at Imageworks, Scott has contributed to *Contact, Starship Troopers, As Good As It Gets, Godzilla, Stuart Little,* and *The Hollow Man.* Prior to that he was employed at Digital Domain, where he worked on *Fifth Element* and *Terminator 2—3D* and did some early R&D on *Titanic.* Other work at previous employers (Metrolight and MotionWorks) includes *Broken Arrow,* a Herbie Hancock music video, an AMC theater spot, and various commercials.

Scott received his B.S. and M.S. in engineering at Harvey Mudd College, where he led student projects for Qualcomm and Hewlett-Packard, including an anti-aliasing research study.

TIM SARNOFF (Executive Vice President and General Manager, Sony Pictures Imageworks) At Sony Pictures Imageworks, Sarnoff is responsible for the overall management of the company.

Prior to Imageworks, Sarnoff was Senior Vice President of Warner Digital Studios, which was established as a division of Time Warner in 1995, after demonstrating the capability of the in-house effects unit with work on *The Little Princess* and *Batman.* In its first year, the division produced visual effects for *Eraser, Mars Attacks,* a *Marvin the Martian* special project, and *Sphere.*

Sarnoff originally joined Warner Bros. in 1989 to help set up Steven Spielberg's *Tiny Toons.* During Sarnoff's tenure, Warner Bros. Animation grew from four to more than three hundred employees, became a separate business unit of Warner Bros., and completed numerous animation projects, including *Tasmania, Batman,* and *Animaniacs.*

He brings an extensive background in production to his post at Imageworks. He began his career as program director for the NBC affiliate, KMIR in Palm Springs, and then served as unit manager for numerous game shows at the NBC network. In 1987 he joined Paramount Television as a manager in their production accounting department, where he not only managed their current slate of shows but also performed the cost analysis for shows being considered.

Mr. Sarnoff is a graduate of Stanford University, where he received his undergraduate degree in 1981.

THE CAST

MICHAEL J. FOX (Voice of Stuart Little)

Michael J. Fox currently stars on the hit ABC series *Spin City* as Deputy Mayor Michael Flaherty. About to begin its fourth season, *Spin City* has already garnered Michael a Golden Globe, a People's Choice Award, and an Emmy nomination for Best Actor.

Fox is well known to television audiences from the hit NBC series *Family Ties,* which ran for seven seasons. Fox won three Emmy Awards and a Golden Globe for his portrayal of the money-obsessed Alex P. Keaton. Fox has also extended his directing talents, having helmed a memorable episode of *Tales from the Crypt.*

Fox's solid filmography includes *Back to the Future* and its successors *Back to the Future II and III,* as well as *The American President, The Frighteners, The Hard Way, The Secret of My Success, Bright Lights Big City, Light of Day, Teen Wolf, Casualties of War, Life With Mikey, For Love or Money,* and *Greedy.*

Born in Edmonton, Alberta, Fox made his professional debut in the CBC situation comedy *Leo and Me.*

Fox lives in New York City with his wife, actress Tracy Pollan, and their three children.

GEENA DAVIS (Mrs. Little)

Geena Davis received an Academy Award® for Best Supporting Actress for her role as the offbeat dog trainer Muriel Pritchett in Lawrence Kasdan's *The Accidental Tourist.*

She was nominated for an Academy Award® and a Golden Globe for her performance as Thelma in Ridley Scott's *Thelma & Louise.* She also received a Golden Globe nomination for Best Actress for her role as a political speech writer in *Speechless,* which she coproduced, and as a baseball phenomenon in *A League of Their Own.*

Making her film debut in *Tootsie,* Davis went on to give memorable performances in *The Fly, Beetlejuice, Earth Girls Are Easy, Quick Change, Hero, Angie, Cutthroat Island,* and *The Long Kiss Goodnight.*

For television, Davis starred in the acclaimed television series *Buffalo Bill* and *Sara.*

Born and raised in Massachusetts, Davis studied acting at New England College and Boston University.

HUGH LAURIE (Mr. Little)

Hugh Laurie emerged from the '81 Cambridge Footlights Review along with castmates Stephen Fry and Emma Thompson. Their award-winning show, *The Cellar Tapes,* aired on the BBC in 1982.

Subsequently, Laurie regularly appeared in Rowan Atkinson's BBC series *The Black Adder.* He also appeared with Stephen Fry on *Saturday Live* for Channel Four, filmed an episode of *Girls on Top* (Central TV), and appeared in the filmed series *Upline* for Channel Four.

Laurie cowrote and performed, with Stephen Fry, the hour-long BBC special *A Bit of Fry and Laurie,* which aired at Christmas and went on to become a long-running television series with a loyal following worldwide.

Laurie also created the uniquely original character Bertie Wooster in the Granada TV series *Jeeves and Wooster* (based on the novels by P. G. Wodehouse), which aired for four seasons and was eventually broadcast in America on PBS.

Laurie's film credits include *Peter's Friends, Sense and Sensibility, 101 Dalmations,* and *Cousin Bette.*

In addition to acting, Laurie is a director, writer, and musician. He has directed various commercials in the United Kingdom and composed and recorded numerous original songs. Four volumes of scripts from *A Bit of Fry and Laurie* have been published.

Laurie recently published his first novel, *The Gun Seller,* to critical acclaim. He has just completed the screenplay of the novel, which will be produced by Russell Smith and John Malkovich's company for United Artists.

JONATHAN LIPNICKI (George)

Eight-year-old Jonathan Lipnicki made his feature-film debut at the age of five in the box office hit *Jerry Maguire.* His endearing portrayal of Ray Boyd earned Lipnicki the 1996 Best Child Performer of the Year Award presented by the National Broadcast Film Critics Association. Most recently his voice was featured in the summer blockbuster *Dr. Dolittle.*

Lipnicki was a series regular on the *Jeff Foxworthy Show* and had the starring role in the CBS series *Meego.*

After wrapping *Stuart Little,* Lipnicki will begin production on location in Scotland on *The Little Vampire,* based on the best-selling books by author Angela Sommer-Bodenburg.

A native Angeleno, Lipnicki lives in Los Angeles with his parents and ten-year-old sister. He enjoys school, particularly studying science, and his hobbies include learning magic, playing the electric guitar, baseball, and studying the martial arts. Lipnicki is a student of Vale Tudo fighting (extreme boxing) and has earned a yellow belt in Brazilian jiu-jitsu.

JULIA SWEENEY (Mrs. Keeper)

To the delight of audiences, Julia Sweeney spent four seasons on *Saturday Night Live* performing a wide range of characters and impersonations, including the sexually ambiguous Pat, singer Ethel Merman, and NBC News's Jane Pauley.

For theater, Sweeney gained critical acclaim in her one-woman theatrical presentation of *God Said Ha!,* an autobiographical portrayal. The film version of *God Said Ha!* was released theatrically by Miramax last year. She also starred as the title role in *Mea's Big Apology,* which garnered the Best Written Play Award from the *L.A. Weekly* (1992) and has been developed by Sweeney into a screenplay.

Sweeney's film credits include *Pulp Fiction; It's Pat; Gremlins II; Honey, I Blew Up the Kids;* and *Coneheads,* and she has appeared in the television series *Mad About You, Baby Boom, Murphy's Law,* and in the telefilm *The Barefoot Executive.*

A native of Spokane, Washington, Sweeney attended the University of Washington in Seattle, graduating with degrees in history and economics. She began working in the entertainment business as an accountant for Columbia Pictures before realizing that acting was her true calling. She was discovered by *Saturday Night Live* producer Lorne Michaels when he saw her perform as part of the Los Angeles comedy troupe The Groundlings.

NATHAN LANE (Voice of Snowbell)

Nathan Lane, born in 1956 in New Jersey, has been a prominent comedic actor in film, on television, and on the stage for two decades. In addition to *Stuart Little,* Lane has lent his voice to the highly successful *The Lion King* and its sequel and the upcoming *Titan AE.* He has worked with a number of the industry's finest actors on such films as *The Birdcage* with Robin Williams; *Mouse Hunt*; Barry Sonnenfeld's *Addams Family Values*; *Joe vs. The Volcano* with Tom Hanks and Meg Ryan; *He Said, She Said,* starring Kevin Bacon; *Ironweed,* starring Meryl Streep; and *Frankie and Johnny,* starring Al Pacino and Michelle Pfeiffer.

Lane also starred in his own sitcom, *Encore, Encore!* and has guest-starred on *Frasier* and *Mad About You.* Lane's upcoming projects include *Popcorn* with Jeff Goldblum and *Love's Labour's Lost* with Kenneth Branagh.

JENNIFER TILLY (Voice of Mrs. Stout)

Jennifer Tilly received both an Academy Award® nomination and an American Comedy Award nomination for Best Supporting Actress for her role as Olive in *Bullets over Broadway.* She also received an American Comedy Award nomination for her performance in *Liar, Liar.*

Tilly was recently seen in the indie feature *Relax, It's Just Sex,* and as Tiffany, Chucky's doll-form companion who is possessed by the spirit of a "bad girl," *in Bride of Chucky.*

Tilly's other film credits include *Bound, The Getaway, Made in America, The Fabulous Baker Boys, Let it Ride,* and *Shadow of the Wolf.*

For television, Tilly starred in the Fox series *Key West* and the ABC series *Shaping Up* as well as Showtime's *Heads,* for which she received a Gemini Award nomination for Best Actress. Recurring television roles included *Hill Street Blues* and appearances on many other series.

Tilly has also won a Theater World Award for her work in Tina Howe's play *One Shoe Off* at the Joseph Papp Theater and a Dramalogue Award for *Vanities.* She has also performed in other stage productions such as *Boy's Life, Tartuffe, Baby with the Bathwater,* and *The Wood Gatherers.*

BRUNO KIRBY (Voice of Mr. Stout)

Bruno Kirby has delighted audiences in both dramatic and comedic roles in such films as *Donnie Brasco; Sleepers; The Basketball Diaries; Golden Gate; City Slickers; When Harry Met Sally . . .; The Freshman; Good Morning Vietnam; Tin Men; We're No Angels; The Godfather, Part II; This Is Spinal Tap;* *Modern Romance; Almost Summer; A Texas Legend; Cinderella Liberty; Between the Lines;* and *The Harrad Experiment.*

For television, Kirby appeared in such telefilms as *Kind of Miracle, A Summer Without Boys, Mastergate, Million Dollar Infield, All My Darling Daughters, Fallen Angels,* and the series *Homicide.* Kirby also directed an episode of *Homicide.*

Kirby starred on Broadway in *Lost in Yonkers* as well as in many other stage productions.

CHAZZ PALMINTERI (Voice of Smokey)

Chazz Palminteri was nominated for a 1995 Academy Award® for Best Supporting Actor for his role in Woody Allen's *Bullets over Broadway.* For that same performance, Palminteri won the Independent Spirit Award for Best Supporting Male and received a SAG Award nomination.

Palminteri's extensive film credits include *Analyze This, Excellent Cadavers, Hurlyburly, A Night at the Roxbury, Mulholland Falls, Faithful, Diabolique, Jade, The Usual Suspects, The Perez Family, The Last Word, A Bronx Tale,* and the forthcoming *Company Man.* He also wrote, produced, directed, and starred in *Dante and the Debutante.*

Palminteri has also written the plays *A Bronx Tale* and *Faithful.*

STEVE ZAHN (Voice of Monty)

Most recently, Zahn was seen in *Out of Sight,* and in October Films' mistaken-identity comedy *Safe Men,* as well as the romantic comedies *You've Got Mail* and *Forces of Nature.*

Zahn next stars in the Miramax comedy *Happy, Texas,* which premiered at the 1999 Sundance Film Festival and earned Zahn a Grand Jury Special Actor Award for his performance. Additionally, Zahn will be seen next year in Miramax's modern-day retelling of *Hamlet,* opposite Ethan Hawke. Currently, Zahn is in production on the dark comedy *Shiny New Enemies.*

Zahn's additional credits include *The Object of My Affection,* and the feature adaptation of Eric Bogosian's play *subUrbia,* reprising the role he created in the Off Broadway production. Zahn also starred in Tom Hanks's directorial debut, *That Thing You Do!* His additional feature credits include roles in *Crimson Tide* and *Race the Sun.*

DAVID ALAN GRIER (Voice of Red)

David Alan Grier will be seen next year in Bonnie Hunt's directorial debut, *Return to Me,* costarring with David Duchovny and Minnie Driver. He recently completed *15 Minutes,* starring Robert De Niro, for director John Herzfeld.

Grier's other feature film credits include *Freeway II: Confessions of a Trickbaby, McHale's Navy, Jumanji, Tales From the Hood, The Player, Boomerang, From the Hip,* and *A Soldier's Story.*

A graduate of the Yale School of Drama, Grier was also seen in the NBC miniseries *The 60s* and the ABC telefilm *A Saintly Switch,* opposite Vivica A. Fox. The actor came to national attention when he starred in the Fox sketch comedy show *In Living Color* from 1990 to 1994.

COLUMBIA PICTURES Presents

A Douglas Wick and
Franklin/Waterman Production

A Film by ROB MINKOFF

Starring:

GEENA DAVIS   HUGH LAURIE   JONATHAN LIPNICKI

Casting by DEBRA ZANE, C.S.A.

Senior Visual Effects Supervisor JOHN DYKSTRA, A.S.C.

Costume Designer JOSEPH PORRO

Music Composed and Conducted by ALAN SILVESTRI

Editor TOM FINAN   Production Designer BILL BRZESKI

Director of Photography GUILLERMO NAVARRO

Executive Producers JEFF FRANKLIN and STEVE WATERMAN
Executive Producer JASON CLARK

Based on the book by E.B. WHITE
Screenplay by M. NIGHT SHYAMALAN and GREG BROOKER

Produced by DOUGLAS WICK   Directed by ROB MINKOFF

CAST

Voice of Stuart Little	Michael J. Fox
Mrs. Little	Geena Davis
Mr. Little	Hugh Laurie
George Little	Jonathan Lipnicki
Voice of Snowbell	Nathan Lane
Voice of Smokey	Chazz Palminteri
Voice of Monty	Steve Zahn
Voice of Lucky	Jim Doughan
Voice of Red	David Alan Grier
Voice of Mr. Stout	Bruno Kirby
Voice of Mrs. Stout	Jennifer Tilly
Voice of Race Announcer	Stan Freberg
Uncle Crenshaw	Jeffrey Jones
Aunt Tina	Connie Ray
Aunt Beatrice	Allyce Beasley
Cousin Edgar	Brian Doyle-Murray
Grandma Estelle	Estelle Getty
Grandpa Spencer	Harold Gould
Uncle Stretch	Patrick O'Brien
Mrs. Keeper	Julia Sweeney
Dr. Beechwood	Dabney Coleman
Anton	Miles Marsico
Officer Sherman	Jon Polito
Officer Allen	Jim Doughan

Race Starter	Joe Bays
Salesman	Taylor Negron
Race Spectator	Kimmy Robertson
Hot Dog Vendor	Tannis Benedict
Skippers	Chuck Blechen
	Westleigh Michael Styer
Boat Registrar	Larry Goodhue
Stunt Coordinator — Animals	Boone Narr
Helicopter Pilot	Al Cerullo
Puppeteers	Guy Himber
	David Kindlon
	Marilee Canaga
	A. Robert Capwell

CREW

Unit Production Manager/Associate Producer	Brian Frankish
Unit Production Manager	D. Scott Easton
First Assistant Director	Benita Allen-Honess
Second Assistant Director	Dieter Busch
CG Animation Supervisor	Henry F. Anderson III
Editor	Julie Rogers
Art Director	Philip Toolin
Assistant Art Director	Shepherd Frankel
Set Decorator	Clay A. Griffith
Script Supervisor	Cariline Davis-Dyer

Camera Operator . . . . Allen D. Easton
B Camera/Steadicam Operator . . . . Harry Garvin
First Assistant Camera . . . . Roberto Blasini
Michael Riba
Second Assistant Camera . . . . Timothy Kane
Camera Loader . . . . Laura C. Holzschuh
Wardrobe Supervisor . . . . Michael Joseph Long
Set Costumer . . . . Deborah Myles Davis
Costumers . . . . Ann Davies Dunn
Nancy Jarzynko
Lisa H. Wong
Key Makeup . . . . Bonita De Haven
Makeup Artist . . . . Mindy Hall
Key Hair . . . . Beth Miller
Hairstylist . . . . Christina Raye
Production Mixer . . . . Mark Ulano, C.A.S.
Boom Operator . . . . Jerome R. Vitucci
Cable . . . . Ross Levy
Video Assist . . . . Ian Kelly
Chief Lighting Technician . . . . David Lee
Assistant Chief Lighting Technician . . . . . Nathan Hathaway
Key Grip . . . . Rick Stribling
Best Boy Grip . . . . Tim Soronen
Dolly Grip . . . . Robert Ivanjack
Rigging Gaffer . . . . Michael Bauman
Best Boy Rigging . . . . Rob Lewbel
Key Rigging Grip . . . . John Warner
Rigging Best Boy . . . . Josh Walters
Special Effects Supervisor . . . . Eric Allard
SPFX Shop . . . . Brent Bell
SPFX Leadman . . . . William Aldridge
SPFX Crew . . . . Tony VanDenecker
Gary Bierend
Larry DeUnger
Eric Dressor
Hans Metz
Production Coordinators . . . . Susan Dukow
Lois A. Walker
Dana Maginnis
Assistant Production Coordinators . . . . Erin Engman
Kika Keith
Shannon Petska
Production Accountant . . . . Denise Morgan McGrath
Assistant Production Accountant . . . . Benjamin Adams

Assistant to Mr. Minkoff . . . . Leah M. Palen
Assistants to Mr. Wick . . . . Nancy Safran
David A. Schreiber
Assistant to Mr. Clark . . . . Warren R. Davis II
Property Master . . . . Tom Tomlinson
Assistant Property Master . . . . Kris Peck
Construction Coordinator . . . . John Samson
Set Designers . . . . Aric Lasher
A. Todd Holland
Stella Vaccaro

Leadmen . . . . Wayne Shepherd
Dugald Stermer
Storyboard Artist . . . . Thomas Jung
Special Consultant . . . . Bruce A. Block
Unit Publicist . . . . Claire S. Raskind
Still Photographer . . . . Peter Iovino
2nd Second Assistant Director . . . . Marisa Ferrey
DGA Trainee . . . . Kent Tsurumaru
Casting Assistant . . . . Terri Taylor
Production Assistants . . . . Annabelle Honess
Julie D. Milstead
Daniel Rodriguez-Wolfson
John Slavin
Christos Vrachnos
Victory Dance Choreographed by . . . . Melinda Buckley
Dialect Coach . . . . Nadia Venesse
Studio Teacher . . . . Susan Reccius

Cats Trained by . . . . . Boone's Animals For Hollywood, Inc.
Animal Trainers . . . . Mark Harden
Shawn Weber
Ursula Brauner
James R. Dew
Susan R. Hanson
Cathy McCallum
Debbie Jacobsohn
David Allsberry
Michelle Iwamoto
Devon Evans

Transportation Captain . . . . Dan Marrow
Tansportation Co-Captain . . . . David R. Diaz

SECOND UNIT

Director . . . . John Dykstra
Unit Production Manager . . . . Dustin Bernard
First Assistant Director . . . . Frederic Roth
Second Assistant Director . . . . David Ascher
Second Unit Director of Photography . . . . Mark Vargo
"A" Camera Operator . . . . Wally Pfister
"B" Camera Operator . . . . Scott Fuller
"A" First Assistant Camera . . . . Bob Hall
"B" First Assistant Camera . . . . Tony Rivetti
"A" Second Assistant Camera . . . . Kevin Ivey
"B" Second Assistant Camera . . . . Philip Shanahan
Script Supervisor . . . . Cassandra Barrere
Production Coordinator . . . . Rebecca Hilliard
Gaffer . . . . Cory Geryak
Best Boy Electric . . . . Larry Sushinski
Key Grip . . . . Jason Newton
Best Boy Grip . . . . Billy Beaird
Dolly Grip . . . . Brian D. Mills
Video Assist . . . . Roger C. Johnson
SPFX Leadman . . . . Richard Stutsman
Propmaster . . . . Michael Hansen
Transportation Co-Captain . . . . Randy Burke

Assistant Editors . . . . Daniel Fort
Odis McKinney
Russell Eaton
Brett Schlaman
Supervising Sound Editor . . . . Lawrence H. Mann
Sound Effects Editors . . . . Suhail Kafity, M.P.S.E.
Steven Ticknor
David Arnold
Duke L. Brown
Voice Over Recording Coordinator . . . . M.K. Susman
Voice Casting . . . . The Reel Team
Supervising Foley Editor . . . . Mark Pappas
Foley Editor . . . . Gary Wright
Supervising ADR Editor . . . . Cindy Marty
ADR Editors . . . . Fred Stafford
Linda Folk
Assistant Sound Editors . . . . Ann Ducommun
Christopher Winter
Foley Artists . . . . Gary Hecker
Michael Broomberg
Foley Mixer . . . . Richard Duarte

Sound Services by Sony Pictures Studios, Culver City, CA

Visual Effects Editors . . . . Linda Drake
Christer Hokanson
Negative Cutting . . . . Conformist, Inc.
Color Timer . . . . Mike Mertens
Re-recording Mixers . . . . Paul Massey
D. M. Hemphill

Main and End Titles Designed by Imaginary Forces

Titles and Opticals by Cinema Research Corporation

Special Visual Effects by Sony Pictures Imageworks

Visual Effects Supervisor . . . . Jerome Chen
Senior Visual Effects Producer . . . . Michelle Murdocca

"Stuart Little" designs fabricated by Sony Pictures Imageworks

SONY PICTURES IMAGEWORKS
Visual Effects Art Director . . . . Martin A. Kline
Creative and Visual Development . . . . . . Thor Freudenthal
Visual Effects Executive Producer . . . . Debbie Denise
Visual Effects Producer . . . . Lydia Bottegoni
Visual Effects Associate Producer . . . . . Audrea Topps-Harjo
Visual Effects Vendor Producer . . . . Jacquie Barnbrook
Visual Effects Marketing Producer . . . . John Clinton
Visual Effects Digital Production Manager . . Jody Echegaray
CG Supervisors . . . . Jim Berney
Bart Giovannetti
Jay K. Redd
Scott Stokdyk

Lead CG Character Animators . . . . Eric Armstrong
Anthony LaMolinara
John Clark Matthews
CG Character Animators . . . . Stephen Baker
Dominick Cercere
Bill Diaz
Paul W. Jessel
Kelvin Lee
Jeff Lin
Jim Moorhead
Sean P. Mullen
Mike Murphy
Dave Mullins
Todd Pilger
Neil Richmond
David Schaub
Alexander E. Sokoloff
Vladimir Todorov
Delio Tramontozzi
Pepe Valencia
David B. Vallone
Todd Wilderman
Additional CG Character Animation . . . . Brad Booker
Jason McDade
Tom Roth
Henry Sato, Jr.
Lead Character Modeller . . . . Kevin Hudson
Character Modellers and
Maquette Sculptors . . . . Thomas R. Dickens
Robin Alan Linn
Michael Sanchez
Look Development/Lighting TD's . . . . Alan Davidson
Rob Engle
Clint Hanson
Robert Winter
Lighting TD's . . . . Judith Adamson
Carol Ashley
Cory Bedwell
Theodore Bialek
Virginia Bowman
Max Bruce
Eric Bruneau
Kiki Candela
Patrick Cohen
Greg Derochie
Jason Dowdeswell
Colin Drobnis
Daniel Eaton
Shine Fitzner
Layne Friedman
Adrian Iler
MacDuff Knox
David C. Lawson
Ben Lishka

Seth Maury
Scott McKee
Kerry Nordquist
Bob Peitzman
Aaron Smith
David A. Smith
Andrew Titcomb
CG Cloth Lead . . . . Mike Travers
CG Cloth TD's . . . . David Allen
Matt Hausman
Rob House
Sho Igarashi
Joshua I. Kolden
John Lee
John Ly
Allen Ruilova
Hector Tantoco
Doug Yoshida
Additional Cloth Development . . . . . . Minds Eye Graphics
Effects Animation Lead . . . . Rob Bredow
Digital Painter . . . . John McGee
CG Animation Support Lead . . . . John McLaughlin
CG Animation Support TD's . . . . Aaron Campbell
Leif Einarrson
Mark Hall
Koji Morihiro
Peter Nofz
Anthony Serenil
Match Move Lead . . . . Rachel Nicoll
Match Move Artists . . . . Bill Ball
Nicole Herr
Joanie Karnowski
Didier Levy
Jeff Smith
David Spencer
Joseph Thomas
David Worman
Alex Whang
Dan Ziegler
PreComp Artist . . . . Tim Llewellyn
Rotoscope Lead . . . . Maura Alvarez
Rotoscope Artists . . . . Loree Perrett
James Valentine
High Speed Compositors . . . . Marguerite Cargill
Kristen Trattner
HSC Production Manager . . . . Thomas F. Ford IV
Visual Effects Coordinators . . . . Amy Adams
Glenn Karpf
Cyndi Ochs
George Stubbs
Visual Effects Assistant Coordinator . . . . Mickey Levy
Visual Effects Production Assistants . . . . . Judah Konigsberg
Eric Scott
Lead Visual Effects Editor . . . . J. W. Kompare

Visual Effects Editor . . . . Deirdre Hepburn-Mangione
Assistant Editor . . . . Steven Rhee
Digital Assistant Editor . . . . John Berri
Negative Lineup . . . . Dee Storm
Video Editor . . . . Ray Wong
Visual Effects Accountant . . . . Robb Miller
Software Engineering Department Manager . . . Chris Russell
Software Supervisor . . . . Amit Agrawal
Lead Software Engineer . . . . Evan Smyth
Software Engineers . . . . Bruce Navsky
Cottalango Loorthu
Armin Bruderlin
Chris Allen
Gilligan Markham
Mike Chmilar
Hiro Miyoshi
Kyle Yamamoto
Sidi Yu
Lead Technical Assistant . . . . Sean Callan
Technical Assistants . . . . Rosendo Salazar
Skye Lyons
Stewart Hoffman
Jeff Dillinger
Apple Peterson
Eric Lebaron
Jason Gyurkovitz

Storyboard/Conceptual Artists . . . . John Bevelheimer
Marzette Bonar
Michael Scheffe
Additional Character Maquette Sculptors . . . Jim McPherson
Brian Wade

Track Readers . . . . Philip E. Phillipson
Brian J. Phillipson
Digital Color Timer . . . . John Nicolard
Assistant Digital Color Timer . . . . Anthony Harris
I/O Supervisor . . . . Dennis Webb
Lead Film Recordist . . . . Derrick Quarles
Lead Scanner Operator . . . . Paul McGhee
Film Recordists . . . . Robert Davis Oh
Chris Arreola
Scanner Operator . . . . Attila Veress
Tape Operator . . . . Brandon England
Senior Systems Engineer . . . . Robert Brophy
Senior Video/Hardware Engineer . . . . Michael Trujillo
Senior Systems Engineers . . . . Benjamin Jacobe
Dean Miya
Systems Engineering Department Manager . . . Alberto Velez
Digital Operations Manager . . . . Andra Bard
Training and Artist Development . . . . Sande Scoredos
Bob Nicoll
Van Phan
Visual Effects Plate Photography Supervisor . . David Stump

Sony Pictures Imageworks
Physical Production Group . . . . John Radulovic
Barry Walton
Brian Wildstein
Darcy Fray
J. J. Linsalata
Allen Mansour
Todd Spencer
Chad Martin
Chris Barker
Mark Christoffersen
Hayden Mounger
Jeff Deyoe
Dan Gindroz
David Cornelius
Peter Collister
Peter Mercurio
Arnaud Peiny
Shane Kelly

THUNDERSTONE MODEL SHOP

Model Shop Supervisor . . . . Phil Notaro
Supervisor . . . . Henry Darnell
Coordinator . . . . Maureen Reggie
Stage Coordinator . . . . Vince Pusateri
Assistant Supervisors . . . . David Emery
Greg Stuhl
Jason Kaufman
Model Makers . . . . Curt Engelmann
Harrison Craig
Donald Sutherland
Mark Weatherbe
Robert Steuer
Richard Slifka
Joshua Culp
Gary Crosby
Edward Turner
Christopher Howard
SPFX Foreman . . . . Brian Marn
SPFX Gang Bosses . . . . Michael Forster
Brad Burbank
SPFX Apprentice . . . . Chris Thornton
Stage Painter Foreman . . . . Thomas O'Brien
Greens Foreman . . . . Bryan McBrien
Sony Imageworks Senior Staff . . . . Jenny Fulle
Tom Hershey
Lincoln Hu
George H. Joblove
Stan Szymanski
Barry Weiss
Tim Sarnoff

CAT VISUAL EFFECTS BY RHYTHM & HUES, INC.

Visual Effects Supervisor . . . . Bill Westenhofer

Visual Effects Producer . . . . Eileen Moran
Senior Lighting Supervisor . . . . Kerry Colonna
Digital Supervisor . . . . Nicholas Titmarsh
Visual Effects Coordinator . . . . Kieran Woo
Visual Effects Assistant Coordinator . . Jennifer Booterbaugh
2D Coordinator . . . . Patrick McCormack
CG Animation Supervisor . . . . Erik de Boer
CG Animators . . . . Ethan Marak
William R. Wright
Jason Ivimey
Mike Stevens
Julius Yang
Hunter Athey
Kevin Bertazzon
Danny Speck
Spyros Tsiounis
Roberto Smith
Dana O'Connor
Davy Crockett Feiten
Raymond Liu
Lighting Supervisor . . . . Betsy Asher Hall
Lighting Leads . . . . Bridget Gaynor
Mike Sandrik
Sandra Voelker
Lighters . . . . Karl Maples
Vandana Konda
Mike Roby
Olivier Barbeau
Arthur Jeppe
Tom Capizzi
Ha Ngan Roda
Gregory Yepes
David Santiago
Caleb Howard
Bradley Sick
Amy Ryan
Pascal Chappuis
Tomas Rosenfeldt
Inferno Artists . . . . Gary Jackemuk
Lyse Beck
2D Supervisor . . . . Craig Seitz
Lead Compositors . . . . Sean MacKenzie
Craig Simms
Jason Greenblum
Ronnie E. Williams Jr.
Match Mover Supervisor . . . . Amy Christensen
Tech Support . . . . Amy Hronek
Visual Effects Editor . . . . Martin November
Visual Effects Assistant Editor . . . . Sharon Smith Holley

CAT VISUAL EFFECTS BY CENTROPOLIS EFFECTS, LLC

Visual Effects Producer . . . . Robin Griffin
Lead CG Character Animator . . . . Benedikt Niemann

CG Character Animators . . . . Steve Harwood
Jordan Harris
Scott Holmes
CG Supervisor . . . . Bret St. Clair
Modeller . . . . Lynn Basas
Lead Fur TD . . . . Nickson Fong
Lead Lighting TD's . . . . Todd Harvey
Leslie Baker
TD's . . . . Michael Addabbo
Daniel Fazel
John Hart
Frederic Soumagnas
Motion Trackers . . . . Michelle Butler
Archie Gogoladze
Compositing Supervisor . . . . Nelson Sepulveda
Compositers . . . . Abra Grupp
Cristin Pescosolido
Conny Fauser-Ruemlin
Paint Supervisor . . . . Robert Cribbett
Paint Artists . . . . Elika Burns
Tom Lamb
Brian Wolf
Visual Effects Coordinator . . . . Tim T. Cunningham
Digital Matte Paintings Provided by . . . . . Illusion Arts, Inc.
Robert Scifo Images
Michele Moen
Animatronic Creatures Supervised by . . . Patrick Tatopoulos

PATRICK TATOPOULOS DESIGNS, INC. CREW
Mechanical Department Supervisor . . . . Guy Himber
Key Mechanical Designer . . . . David Kindlon
Mechanics . . . . A. Robert Capwell
Samara Hagopian
Production Accountant . . . . Julie Mankowski
Art Director . . . . Oana Bogdan
Fabrication Supervisor . . . . Marilee Canaga
Fabrication Technician . . . . Carol Jones
Foam Supervisor . . . . Todd Heindel
Hair Supervisor . . . . Lisa Codero
Key Moldmaker . . . . Gary Pawlowski
Key Painter . . . . Eric Harris

Filmed at Sony Pictures Studios, Culver City, California

Music Supervisor . . . . Elliot Lurie
Orchestrations by . . . . William Ross
Bruce Babcock
Mark McKenzie
Conrad Pope
Score Recorded and Mixed by . . . . Dennis Sands
Assistant to Composer . . . . David Bifano
Music Editor . . . . Kenneth Karman
Assistant Music Editor . . . . Jacqueline Tager

Soundtrack on Motown/Universal Records

MUSIC

"Walking Tall"
Written by Burt Bacharach and Tim Rice
Produced by Burt Bacharach and Elliot Lurie
Performed by Lyle Lovett   Courtesy of Curb/MCA Records

"That's Amore"
Written by Jack Brooks and Harry Warren
Performed by Dean Martin   Courtesy of Capitol Records
Under license from EMI-Capitol Music Special Markets

"If You Can't Rock Me"
Written by Brian Setzer   Produced by Peter Collins
Performed by The Brian Setzer Orchestra
Courtesy of Interscope Records

"1+1=2"
Written by Lou Bega, Zippy, D. Fact and Frank Lio
Performed by Lou Bega
Courtesy of BMG Ariola Muenchen GmbH

"You're Where I Belong"
Written by Diane Warren   Produced by Keith Thomas
Performed by Trisha Yearwood
Courtesy of MCA Records Nashville

The Major League Baseball trademarks depicted in this motion picture were licensed by Major League Baseball Properties, Inc. Plush toys courtesy of Gund, Inc. © Gund, Inc. Barbie® Dolls & Hot Wheels® Cars courtesy of Mattel, Inc. Lenox Brands

Special Thanks to: The NYC Mayor's Office of Film, Theatre & Television Broadcasting

Color by CFI   Prints by Deluxe®

COLUMBIA PICTURES
A SONY PICTURES ENTERTAINMENT COMPANY

ACKNOWLEDGMENTS

There are many people, past and present, who deserve credit for their contribution to *Stuart Little* and the creative team. In some small way, this volume attempts to celebrate many of the individuals who brought their creative energy to bear on this project. Undoubtedly, there will be many others whose individual work is portrayed as part of the collective whole. There are credits at the end of the movie and in the pages of this book. Beside every title there is a name and those names each represent a person without whose effort and talent neither this film nor this chronicle would have been possible. I hope that you will join us in acknowledging them.

Books such as this do not just happen. It is a combination of hunting and gathering, an almost primal impulse to bring together the fruit of these labors. To people like Holly Haines, the photo editor for *Stuart Little* in Columbia Pictures Worldwide Marketing, we say thank you. Of the thousands of images produced for each movie, no other film project has been quite like this one. Holly grasped long before the first frames were ever shot how different this film would be and worked tirelessly throughout the process to ensure that great images would be available for the world to see and share the experience of making this movie. To Kika Keith, who has been an invaluable asset in sifting through the mountains of production material to produce some of the gems in this book. To Jamie Geller Hawtof, Dana Precious, Bob Levin, and Ed Russell, and their teams in New York and Los Angeles, your taste, style, and integrity make you and this project very special.

To Executive Producer Jason Clark, who has been a champion of this book from the day it was first proposed, and to Producer Doug Wick and Rob Minkoff for your support. Were it not for the three of you and your vision of what *Stuart Little* could be, neither this book nor this movie would have been. A note of thanks should also be extended to your tireless assistants. To executives like Amy Pascal, Lori Furie, Lucy Fisher, Gareth Wigan, and Gary Martin, who shared their wisdom throughout this project and offered invaluable comments in their reading of the text.

A special thank-you goes to Linda Sunshine, who pulled this amorphous material together and made sense of it all. It was exciting to watch Linda become absorbed in the magic of creating *Stuart*. And thank you to Esther Margolis and her staff at Newmarket Press for taking on this book.

To the hardware and software producers whose products form the backbone of our enterprise, we gratefully acknowledge your ingenuity. Through collaboration there is almost no limit.

To Tim Sarnoff for having the chutzpah to say that we not only could do this, but should do this project. That single act changed a whole company. To Ken Ralston, Imageworks' President, for his artistic vision and continued amazement at the quality of the work. And no acknowledgment would be complete without Kenneth S. Williams, President of Sony Pictures Entertainments' Digital Studios Division. His trusted counsel and steady hand on the tiller has enabled Imageworks and the other technology-driven businesses of his division to grow and thrive in this dynamic environment.

Perhaps the biggest thank-you goes to the readers, for it is your interest and appreciation for the art and science that inspires the process of creativity. Thank you for being.

—DON LEVY
Executive Director Marketing and Communications